THE ECONOMICS OF INTERNATIONAL ADJUSTMENT

THE ECONOMICS OF INTERNATIONAL ADJUSTMENT

EDITED BY RANDALL HINSHAW

THE JOHNS HOPKINS PRESS:
BALTIMORE AND LONDON

Manufactured in the United States of America
The Johns Hopkins Press, Baltimore, Maryland 21218
The Johns Hopkins Press Ltd., London
Library of Congress Catalog Card Number 78-127351
ISBN 0-8018-1204-6

TO THE MEMORY OF
ARTHUR GARDINER COONS
1900-1968

CONTENTS

CONTRIBUTORS

SIDNEY S. ALEXANDER, Professor of Economics, Massachusetts Institute of Technology

ROBERT Z. ALIBER, Professor of Economics, Graduate School of Business, University of Chicago

WILLIAM R. ALLEN, Chairman, Department of Economics, University of California, Los Angeles

C. FRED BERGSTEN, Economic Adviser, National Security Council

EDWARD M. BERNSTEIN, President, EMB (Ltd.), Research Economists

ARTHUR I. BLOOMFIELD, Professor of Economics, University of Pennsylvania

ALICE BOURNEUF, Professor of Economics, Boston College

W. RANDOLPH BURGESS, Undersecretary of the Treasury, 1955-57

RICHARD N. COOPER, Professor of Economics, Yale University

GORDON K. DOUGLASS, Chairman, Department of Economics, Pomona College

HOWARD S. ELLIS, Flood Professor of Economics Emeritus, University of California, Berkeley

P. T. ELLSWORTH, Visiting Professor of Economics, University of California, Riverside

JOHN EXTER, Senior Vice President, First National City Bank of New York

RICHARD N. GARDNER, Henry L. Moses Professor of Law and International Relations, Columbia University

GOTTFRIED HABERLER, Galen L. Stone Professor of International Trade, Harvard University

ALVIN H. HANSEN, Littauer Professor of Political Economy Emeritus, Harvard University

SEYMOUR E. HARRIS, Littauer Professor of Political Economy Emeritus, Harvard University

SIR ROY HARROD, Oxford University

MICHAEL A. HEILPERIN, Professor of Economics, Long Beach State College

RANDALL HINSHAW, Professor of Economics, Claremont Graduate School

CONRAD C. JAMISON, Vice President and Economist, Security Pacific National Bank

FRITZ MACHLUP, Walker Professor of Economics and International Finance, Princeton University

LLOYD A. METZLER, Professor of Economics, University of Chicago

ROBERT A. MUNDELL, Professor of Economics, University of Chicago

Robert Oliver, Professor of Economics, California Institute of Technology

Gardner Patterson, Assistant Director-General, GATT, Geneva

Walter S. Salant, Senior Fellow, The Brookings Institution

Paul A. Samuelson, Professor of Economics, Massachusetts Institute of Technology

Leonard S. Silk, Chairman, Board of Editors, Business Week, 1967-69

Robert Solomon, Adviser to the Board and Director, Division of International Finance, Board of Governors of the Federal Reserve System

Frank A. Southard, Jr., Deputy Managing Director, International Monetary Fund

Willard L. Thorp, Assistant Secretary of State for Economic Affairs, 1946-52

Robert Triffin, Frederick William Beinecke Professor of Economics, Yale University

Henry C. Wallich, Professor of Economics, Yale University

Arthur N. Young, International Financial Adviser

John Parke Young, Former Chief, Division of International Finance, U.S. Department of State

FOREWORD

Nearly forty eminent experts in international economics assembled in March 1969 to participate in the Claremont International Monetary Conference, sponsored by Claremont Graduate School in cooperation with the other Claremont Colleges. The conference continued an inquiry begun at the Johns Hopkins conference of January 1967 in Bologna, Italy. At Bologna, the focus was on gold in relation to international monetary reform, a theme which suggested the more basic question, pursued at Claremont, of "international adjustment"—that is to say, the question of how countries can deal with their external payments problems without needlessly jeopardizing their other economic objectives. This book on the Claremont conference, edited by Professor Randall Hinshaw of Claremont Graduate School, can be regarded as a companion volume to the book based on the Bologna conference, *Monetary Reform and the Price of Gold* (Baltimore: The Johns Hopkins Press, 1967), also edited by Professor Hinshaw, who, as a visiting professor at The Johns Hopkins Bologna Center, organized the Bologna gathering.

The Claremont conference was chaired with distinction by Willard L. Thorp, with Fritz Machlup gallantly agreeing on short notice to serve as moderator, a role Lord Robbins had ably performed at the Bologna conference and had been invited to repeat at Claremont. It is a sign of the times that Lord Robbins' attendance at the Claremont meeting was at the last minute prevented by the student crisis at the London School of Economics, of which he is Chairman of the Court of Governors. The conferees at Claremont likewise were treated to a student demonstration of a peaceful kind—a rally on behalf of the installation of a Black Studies Center at the Claremont Colleges. Thus the flavor of the college epoch through which we are passing was preserved and to some extent heightened by the choice of an American college campus as the location for such a gathering. The conference itself proceeded entirely peacefully. A large number of students, both graduate and undergraduate, were privileged to attend as observers the sessions held in Balch Hall on the Scripps College campus. A felicitous link with the Bologna conference was the participation, as a distinguished observer, of C. Grove Haines, Director of the Bologna Center of The Johns Hopkins University.

Generous financial support was graciously granted in equal amounts by The John Randolph Haynes and Dora Haynes Foundation of Los Angeles and by Security Pacific National Bank. Additional funds were provided by the firms of Bateman Eichler, Hill Richards, Inc., and P & X Markets, Inc.

Randall Hinshaw once again acted as organizer and secretary of the conference, and gave it enormous quantities of time and devotion. We, his colleagues, are grateful to him and to the eminent economists who made the conference so distinguished an event. While the list of all those who contributed to the success of the gathering would be long indeed, it would be ungrateful of us not to acknowledge the many hours of assistance given by Francis H. Lindley, Chairman of the Board of the Haynes Foundation; Conrad C. Jamison, Vice President and Economist of Security Pacific National Bank; John Parke Young, noted southern California economist; Betty Jane Combs, Director of Special Events at Scripps College; Margaret Brocher, Secretary of the Claremont Graduate Faculty in Economics; and Timothy Connor, graduate student, who organized an efficient student transportation service for the convenience of the conferees.

A poignant and appropriate note for the conference is reflected in its dedication to the memory of a distinguished Californian, Arthur G. Coons. As Chairman of the Committee on Research and Grants of the Haynes Foundation, Dr. Coons, who died on July 25, 1968, had been keenly interested and actively involved in planning the forthcoming meeting. For twenty years, he had served as President of Occidental College and, before that, was himself an outstanding economist and professor at Claremont Graduate School. His presence at the conference was sorely missed and his name affectionately remembered.

LOUIS T. BENEZET
President
Claremont Graduate School

Randall Hinshaw

CHAPTER I

INTRODUCTION

This book owes its origin to the second of two closely related conferences on international monetary questions. The first, held in Italy at the Bologna Center of The Johns Hopkins University in January 1967, was concerned with the role of gold, and particularly the price of gold, in international monetary reform.* Participating were the authors of the three leading approaches to reform—Edward M. Bernstein, Jacques Rueff, and Robert Triffin—who debated their respective positions in the presence of a group of eminent specialists in international economics.

The emphasis of the Bologna gathering was on international liquidity, an emphasis which prompted Professor J. E. Meade of Cambridge University to make one of the more memorable statements of the conference. "I feel very sincerely and very strongly," he said, "that the attention given to liquidity in our discussions is quite out of proportion to the attention that has been given to adjustment. I am saddened at the sight of so many people in such positions of great responsibility, and in such positions of intellectual and academic influence in these matters, spending such a high proportion of time discussing the differences—which I admit are very important—between the various ways of controlling and increasing international liquidity, relative to the proportion of time which they have given to what in my view is the much more important problem of how the countries in the free world—the developed, industrialized, liberal countries of the Atlantic community, if you like—adjust their payments to each other."

These sentiments fell on far from unsympathetic ears.

*A book on the Bologna conference was published under the title *Monetary Reform and the Price of Gold: Alternative Approaches* (Baltimore: The Johns Hopkins Press, 1967), ed. Randall Hinshaw.

Rueff agreed that international adjustment was "the main question," and Lord Robbins, the moderator, in summarizing the conference dialogue, remarked that he had "been struck by Monsieur Rueff's continual emphasis on the adjustment problem" and by "the agreement of Messrs. Triffin and Bernstein on the necessity for adjustment and for continuous adjustment." Bernstein, in fact, had remarked that "in a sense" adjustment "is the most important question, because the only reason for having a discussion on reserves is to make adjustment easier." Before the end of the Bologna meeting, another participant, John Parke Young, suggested in a corridor conversation that a subsequent conference be devoted exclusively to the theme of international adjustment. His idea led directly to the Claremont International Monetary Conference of March 1969, which addressed its attention to exactly that theme.

Participating in the three-day Claremont conference were between thirty and forty of the leading authorities in the international monetary field, including several of the key figures in the Bologna gathering. Great effort was made to assure that the conference would be as spontaneous and creative as possible. No formal papers were presented; instead, a tape recording was made of the entire meeting. To take maximum advantage of the assembled talent, the first day was devoted to an exploration of the central issues in international adjustment. Each participant was invited to make a brief statement setting forth his own assessment of the primary issues, and, on the basis of these statements, the members agreed to devote the second day to a dialogue on exchange-rate issues and the third day to a dialogue on adjustment questions outside the exchange-rate field. As would be expected, these dialogues were of rare quality, and an important element in their success was the impressive skill of Willard L. Thorp as chairman and of Fritz Machlup as moderator.

Fortunately, the Claremont conference came at a time when interest was shifting from questions of reform to questions of adjustment. With respect to reform, two important steps had been taken since the Bologna conference. The first was the agreement in September 1967 by members of the International Monetary Fund on a proposal to establish a new international reserve asset in the form of "Special

Drawing Rights" (SDR's), the purpose being to promote an appropriate and orderly growth in the total volume of international monetary reserves. The second step, designed to deal with a rapidly developing gold crisis, was the agreement of March 1968 preserving the official $35 price for gold and removing the link between official and private gold transactions, thereby putting an end to the alarming movement of gold from the official to the private sector during the first quarter of the year. These two developments were, at least, provisional answers to the questions of what to do about international liquidity and about the price of gold, and it was natural that attention should shift to problems of international adjustment, which unfortunately still abounded.

Of particular interest and concern were problems in the field of exchange-rate policy. Between the Bologna conference and the Claremont conference had occurred the sterling crisis of November 1967, resulting in a 14 percent devaluation of sterling, and a franc crisis stemming from unfavorable wage and price developments following the French student uprisings in the spring of 1968. While the franc had not yet been devalued, there was a widespread feeling that devaluation could not be long avoided, and there was also a widespread conviction that, in view of the large persistent surplus in the German balance of payments, an upward revaluation of the mark was badly needed—not least in the interest of the dollar, long in a vulnerable position because of the continuing U. S. payments deficit. Both a devaluation of the franc and an appreciation of the mark were to occur before the end of the year. In the meantime, there was a growing interest, both in academic and in official circles, in exploring certain innovations in exchange-rate policy—notably the proposals for a "wider band" and for a "sliding parity," both aimed at achieving greater exchange-rate flexibility. This growing interest in taking a new look at the case for greater flexibility of exchange rates was strongly revealed in the Claremont conference, which included members from both academic and official headquarters.

Without getting into technical details, it may be helpful at this point to consider, in the broadest possible terms, the role of exchange-rate policy in international adjustment—not in the abstract, but in the actual world of the 1970's. Having spent many weeks becoming exceedingly familiar with the transcript of the conference tape recording, I offer the ensuing observations, not as a summary of the wisdom distilled from the Claremont dialogue—and certainly not as the "last word," a privilege properly reserved for the moderator—but as a few broad personal conclusions, as reinforced or modified after long and strong exposure to the views of a group of able and wise experts.

International adjustment always takes place in some fashion, but this statement offers little more comfort than the observation that an airplane always gets back to the ground somehow. For adjustment can be a wretchedly painful affair. What is wanted, of course, is adjustment with minimum pain and with minimum impairment of economic efficiency. Ideally, for countries in external deficit, this means adjustment without unemployment and without recourse to import restrictions which shelter high-cost production or to capital controls which interfere with the most efficient international allocation of capital resources. For countries in external surplus, adjustment without pain means, in particular, adjustment without inflation.

International monetary reform can assist adjustment by providing an orderly growth in international liquidity and by removing the threat of sharp and capricious contractions in global reserves. A notable example of reform reducing an adjustment problem is the gold agreement of March 1968, which, by stopping a hemorrhage of gold from the official to the private sector, greatly reduced the gravity of U.S. payments difficulties, and shunted aside, at least for the time being, unwise government proposals for dealing with those difficulties by new forms of control. But monetary reform by itself is no substitute for adjustment; on the contrary, increased liquidity, by postponing the day of reckoning, may transform a minor adjustment problem into one ultimately calling for Procrustean measures.

My next observation is that the United States, as a "giant among nations" (to use Peter Kenen's phrase) and as custodian of the leading international means of payment, has a unique responsibility, not so much to keep its international accounts continuously in balance, as to keep its commodity price level as stable as possible. This point has often been made by Robert Mundell, and I wholeheartedly agree. I would add that the conclusion has a direct bearing on the issue of fixed versus flexible exchange rates. Few would quarrel with the proposition that, in a world in which the United States and other countries were successful in maintaining a high degree of price stability, fixed exchange rates could be easily maintained and adjustment problems could be easily handled, without recourse to unemployment or restrictions, by an appropriate "mix" of fiscal and monetary policy. Of course, for any countries not maintaining internal price stability, the proposition would not be true, and the case for flexible exchange rates is often stated in terms of the adjustment problems of those particular countries.

But a much more interesting case concerns the country which is sufficiently wise and enlightened to be able to maintain domestic price stability, full employment, and a healthy growth rate in a world in which *other* countries, including particularly the United States, are failing to prevent a steady rise in the domestic commodity price level. This is the sort of world in which we have recently been living, and, in such a world, a country which succeeds in maintaining internal price stability will find itself in a position of steadily increasing external surplus if it maintains a fixed exchange rate. From its total national product, successively larger slices will have to be made available to the foreign sector, whether financed by loans, by gifts, or by an inflow of monetary reserves (the growth of which will pose an increasingly difficult problem for the central bank if the price level is to remain stable). Indeed, to maintain internal price stability and a fixed exchange rate under such conditions, the country must be content to "absorb" a declining fraction of current output; in other words, there must be a gradual decline in the total of goods and services available to the home population, unless—as is unlikely—the national product, because of increasing productivity, is growing so rapidly that an actual decline is unnecessary.

What should such a country do? I entirely agree with those who hold that the most sensible policy would be, by one technique or another, to let the country's exchange rate gradually move upward—indefinitely, if necessary, and in any case as long as there is an excess demand for the country's currency. Why? Because the rising exchange rate would prevent the stable internal price level from getting out of line with the rising price structure abroad, and thus would remove the tendency toward external surplus. The country no longer would have to content itself with a diminishing fraction of its current output in order to maintain a stable price level.

Of course, there are those who would respond that the same problem can be handled under the present "adjustable peg" system by means of occasional upward changes in parity. But a flexible rate seems decidedly superior to intermittent revaluations in this situation for two main reasons. In the first place, the country avoids being exposed to massive inflows of "hot money" in anticipation of revaluation and then being exposed—after revaluation has taken place—to massive outflows of funds occasioned by the natural desire of speculators to realize their profits. Such capital movements added greatly to German problems before and after the revaluation of the mark in October 1969. In the second place—and even more important—a continuous adjustment through a flexible exchange rate would prevent exporters from developing a larger stake in the foreign market than can be sustained under equilibrium conditions. Currency appreciation is understandably opposed by exporters in situations where a large payments surplus has developed, because it may mean a sharp contraction in sales abroad. But where the exchange rate is free to rise, so that a surplus position never develops, exporters do not acquire an abnormally large stake in the foreign market, and thus need not suffer a decline in foreign sales as the exchange rate gradually inches upward.

This leads me to a brief remark on sharing the so-called burden of adjustment. Central bankers and finance ministers in countries tending to be in external surplus are fond of saying that it is unfair to ask their countries to bear the "burden" of adjustment, since their surpluses are caused by the mistakes of others and not by their own. But this observation seems to me curiously mercantilistic. The country with an expanding surplus not only does the rest of the world a favor by letting its exchange rate rise; it does itself a favor by effectively dealing with inflationary pressures without the need for progressively more stringent fiscal and monetary policies to assure the steady contraction in domestic expenditure that would be required if the exchange rate remained unchanged. Particularly will it be doing itself a favor if it does not *delay* exchange-rate action, since, by avoiding a surplus, the country will not acquire an unsustainably large interest in the export market.

While much more can and should be said on this subject, it would be unfair to intrude further into a discussion in which exchange-rate questions received such detailed and expert consideration. Instead, a word about the plan of the book. Except for the Introduction, the book is a lightly edited transcription of the tape recording made of the entire conference. The statements appear in the order in which they were made, and no statements on the conference theme have been omitted. In Chapter II, the opening remarks of the chairman and the moderator are presented, as well as the immediately ensuing statements of Edward M. Bernstein and Robert Triffin, who, as key figures in the Bologna conference, were asked to provide a transition to the Claremont conference theme. Chapter III contains the opening statements of conference members setting forth their evaluation of the central issues in international adjustment. The dialogue on exchange-rate policy appears in Chapter IV, followed by a dialogue on other adjustment questions in Chapter V. The final chapter is devoted to the concluding observations of the moderator, Fritz Machlup.

Willard L. Thorp, Fritz Machlup,
Edward M. Bernstein, Robert Triffin

CHAPTER II

INTERNATIONAL ADJUSTMENT: ISSUES AND OPTIONS

Chapters II and III are concerned with the first day of the Claremont conference, a day devoted entirely to an exploration of the central issues in international adjustment. The present chapter includes the opening remarks of the chairman, Willard L. Thorp, and of the moderator, Fritz Machlup, followed by statements of two of the leading members of the preceding Bologna conference, Edward M. Bernstein and Robert Triffin, linking the theme of the earlier conference—international monetary reform—with the Claremont theme of adjustment. Chapter III contains the ensuing discussion on key issues by other members of the Claremont conference. The statements in both chapters are presented in the order in which they were delivered. As an eminent economist, Chairman Thorp participated actively in the discussion, and his observations, reactions, and obiter dicta are included throughout the book.

R. H.

Chairman THORP: To me it is interesting that we should need to assemble to talk about international adjustment. The subject is one which economists have struggled with since the earliest days and which they have devised their most handsome theories about. Yet here we are with this ancient subject, knowing at the outset that we don't agree about the character of the problem as it presents itself today or about the relative effectiveness of the various ways of dealing with it. Therefore, one of the most important things for us to do in these few sessions is to clarify, as far as we can, exactly why we disagree. To be sure, many of those around this table have put forth in elaborate detail their attitudes on this or that part of the subject. We should take this opportunity to find out why they have not convinced the world—or, for that matter, all of us—that they have solutions to the problems we shall be discussing.

I suppose that there is not even agreement on what the objective is or on what kind of balance we are talking about.

Are we in balance if there is an accumulation of claims against the United States? Should our counterclaims be considered? Should getting the U. S. deficit within an annual total of $2 billion be regarded as a success or should the aim be zero? And where should the pressure be applied? The moment we ponder about what the various numbers actually mean, we become involved in all sorts of institutional questions.

One of our main difficulties is that our world is vastly more complicated than the neat and tidy world in which earlier theories were developed. To take only one recent example, the birth and rapid growth of the Eurodollar market has complicated the interpretation of the balance of payments. Not long ago, when I was Chairman of the OECD [Organization for Economic Cooperation and Development] Development Assistance Committee, we struggled in Paris with the problem of who, in reality, is exporting capital to the less developed countries when an American businessman borrows in the Eurodollar market in order to invest in some foreign country. Whose capital is going where, and what country should get the credit for it? This is merely one of the new problems that are bothering us all.

Now a word about procedure. It seems that the most useful thing to do at this early stage would be to spend some time exchanging views on exactly what each of us thinks are the key problems in international adjustment. We have little time and must select those problems on which we should try to get some sort of understanding or agreement. But we could waste time talking at cross purposes unless we first come into some sort of focus. Therefore, we are commencing this morning with somewhat more elaborate and comprehensive analyses by three of our members. When they have finished, I hope that everyone will find his spirit moving him to comment on what he feels are the central problems in this field, realizing full well that the minute we talk about international adjustment we are also involved in the problems of domestic adjustment.

To begin, I will now ask our able moderator, Fritz Machlup, to moderate. Webster says that "to moderate" is "to reduce violence" and "to keep within bounds." How better could we get started?

FRITZ MACHLUP: Thank you, Mr. Chairman. I shall try to

follow your instructions, but I should confess that I once called myself an "immoderator," because I sometimes like to exaggerate and to provoke. I shall try, however, to resist that temptation and to be all that a good moderator should be.

It is difficult for me to talk about international adjustment without first saying a few words about the institutional background. Anyone who has had occasion to talk to bankers or to other practical men in the world of finance, whether they are in government or in business, will recognize that there is a very peculiar type of conservative who detests and opposes change as long as it is proposed or discussed, but who fails to notice change once it has happened. Since 1947 there have been enormous changes in international monetary arrangements; yet these people continue to insist that nothing should be changed in the monetary system. It is of course difficult to say, when several important changes have occurred, whether the "system" is, or is no longer, the same system. While the answer is largely a matter of definition, I would not hestitate, on the basis of my own conception, to say that we have had, not one system, but at least four or five systems in the last twenty-four years.

To illustrate, we have moved from inconvertibility to convertibility and then back to restrictions on convertibility, particularly in the sector of capital transactions. As another example, we have moved from a two-tier price for gold to a unified price and then, in March 1968, back to a two-tier system. Moreover, the convertibility of the dollar into gold, at the central-bank level, now means something quite different from what it meant a few years ago. Call it a "gentlemen's agreement" or whatever you wish; my friend, Triffin, speaks of "negotiated holdings of reserves." I could mention numerous other developments, including the rapid evolution of the Eurodollar market, which have radically altered the international monetary environment and have made it absolutely meaningless to speak of the existing system as if it were the same system we had two decades ago. The moral of all this is that we shouldn't be afraid of change, since we've lived through so much of it already, though, of course, we should make every effort to assure that any change in existing arrangements is in the right direction.

This observation leads me directly to our theme of international adjustment, which I would first like to relate to the payments position of the United States—a position, I think, of serious maladjustment. For the last three years, we have had a rate of price inflation in the United States which makes the situation worse. Some people belive that ending the inflation would solve the problem. I can only say that I wish it were so, but I doubt it. When a demand inflation raises the price level in the United States above the price levels in other countries, stopping the inflation does not remove the price differentials. At fixed exchange rates, that gap can be closed only by a decline in the domestic price level or by a rise in price levels abroad.

A decline in the American price level is not to be expected, and no one really wants it. At the same time, a sufficient price inflation in Europe—particularly in Germany and Italy, the two countries with the largest payments surpluses—seems also not too likely, especially when we are told that Germany intends to keep its price level from rising more than 1 or 2 percent a year. Since we would be happy to slow down the increase of our price level to 3 percent a year, I fail to see how a disinflation in the United States would correct the large maladjustment that now exists.

If disinflation in the United States is no cure, what else can be done? I believe that the price adjustments we need are likely to require changes in exchange rates. And that brings me to the subject of exchange-rate flexibility. Let me first make it clear that I don't think we will ever have completely flexible exchange rates. We can talk about the advantages of free flexibility until we are blue in the face, but the monetary authorities of the world simply won't go along. Perhaps they have their reasons. But, while freely fluctuating rates are out, the possibility of greater exchange-rate flexibility than we have now cannot be dismissed as an impractical idea, particularly since some of the men in charge of monetary affairs have changed their tune considerably in the last few years—and especially in the last few months. People who have always rejected even the modest proposal for a wider band around parity now say, "Well, maybe this ought to be studied." Such studies have actually been started in a number of government departments, in several central banks, and in international organizations.

Greater exchange-rate flexibility raises many questions, and we might first list some of the objections raised by the opposition. One assertion is that greater flexibility, whether in the form of a wider band or of a gliding adjustment (the so-called crawling peg), would lead to a considerable increase in speculation and that the speculation would be of the destabilizing rather than the stabilizing variety. Another claim is that exchange-rate variations within a band, or with a crawl of the peg, would lead to an enormous demand for forward cover—much greater than under the present system of jumping exchange rates. (I distinguish between gliding rates and jumping rates; these are the only alternatives.) According to a third argument, this increased demand for forward cover could not be met by forward markets, at least not under present institutions. A fourth proposition states that any increase in forward cover that could be provided would entail a huge increase in the cost to be borne by hedgers. A fifth assertion is that this increase in cost, or in uncovered risk, or both, would lead to a reduction in international trade as well as in international capital movements. These are the main propositions that have come to my attention, and they seem sufficiently plausible to call for more inquiry.

On another plane, a question that has long puzzled me is how we can make the transition to greater flexibility. If we want wider bands or gliding parities, is it possible to start from the present parities, or should there first be a realignment, where parities are particularly far out of line? Would we not inaugurate the system of greater flexibility under the worst possible conditions if we started from badly misaligned exchange rates? On the other hand, would not the jumps in parities that are needed for a good start of the new system be so difficult to achieve that we would never get to any start at all? I raise these questions for your consideration, and do not propose at this stage to give you the answers.

The proposal for a wider band also raises questions concerning the transition. In view of our lack of experience with a wider band, should we try out the system quite cautiously by widening the band only by a very modest amount? Some of the operators at the foreign-exchange desks of the large commercial banks are willing to give the wider band a try, but they say, "Please, let's not begin by widening the band to 4 or 5 percent on either side of parity; let's go to 2 or 2¼ percent and see what happens." Should we accept this approach? It would have the advantage, I believe, of allaying a lot of anxiety. The operators might then see that nothing terrible would happen, that the sky would not fall, and that they could easily cope with the new regime. On the other hand, the main advantage of a wider band—namely, of allowing adjustment of the real flow of goods and services—would hardly be forthcoming, because if we permitted only a 2 percent deviation from parity, we could not expect much of an effect on the trade balance; the effect might be considerable if we had the possibility of a 4 or 5 percent deviation. Thus, if the practical people in government and in the central banks should agree to widen the band to, say, 2 percent on either side of parity, I am not certain whether we should accept the offer. I say this because everything going wrong after such a limited reform would be blamed on the new system—and with too little flexibility much could, indeed, go wrong.

Let me now return to the subject of the crawling peg. Here we need a great deal more exploration. Among the questions that immediately occur to me are the following: Assuming that agreement is reached on the principle of a gliding parity, should the peg crawl on the basis of a fixed formula derived from past behavior or should it crawl in a manner determined by discretion? If by discretion, what rules or criteria should govern the discretion? Is discretion likely to lead to competitive depreciation? These are just a few of the questions that need our attention; and, again, I shall refrain at this stage from offering ready-made answers.

I would like to conclude by saying a few more words about the payments disequilibrium of the United States. We all know that our surplus on official settlements in 1968 was a fluke in the sense that several items were either reversible or not sustainable. So there is still a distinct maladjustment. The trade balance is particularly distressing; the trade surplus is the lowest in thirty years, amounting to only $600 million in 1968. I believe that a country as rich as the United States should have a normal capital outflow of at least 1 percent of the gross national product. That would call for a trade surplus, or rather a positive balance on goods and services, of at least $8 billion a year. This we don't begin to have. By way of contrast, the Germans have a trade surplus of between $4 billion and $5 billion, which—as Bob Solomon and I estimated last night—is between 3 and 4 percent of their GNP; and they consider that normal (though I don't). Now, if a country like Germany expects to have a long-term capital outflow of 3 percent of its GNP, should the United States have a zero outflow of capital? Or perhaps even an inflow of capital? Occasionally, perhaps, but in the long run it makes no sense to me, and, on this basis, I would say that we are in a position of severe maladjustment. I have no objection to calling it a fundamental disequilibrium, and I have no hesitation in saying that adjustment has to come.

Chairman THORP: Thank you, Fritz. This conference, as you all know, is a sequel to the conference on gold and international monetary reform held at Bologna in 1967. Our moderator has referred to problems of transition, which leads me to propose as the next item on the agenda a brief transition period, in which we ask two distinguished participants of the Bologna conference, Edward M. Bernstein and Robert Triffin, to assist us in making the transition from the theme of the earlier conference to our own theme of international adjustment. I shall call first on Eddie Bernstein.

EDWARD M. BERNSTEIN: Taking as my starting point the remarks of Fritz Machlup, I will begin by saying that I agree with him on a most important point. The international monetary system that we have today is not the system we introduced in 1947, much less the system that prevailed before. This is the very beauty of the Bretton Woods approach. Bretton Woods established, as an everyday occurrence, international monetary cooperation. It eased the process of evolution. But while the system has gone through many changes, it has remained sufficiently the same so that we can still speak of it as an international monetary system. Indeed, in those aspects that I want to discuss, the system has not changed greatly since 1947.

The International Monetary Fund starts with the principle that it would be in the interest of individual countries, and of the world economy as a whole, to have a balanced pattern of international payments—which means that the great trading countries, averaging good years and bad, should keep their surpluses and deficits about equal. This, of course, raises the question of what we mean by a surplus or a deficit, but for a country like the United States, I would certainly say that the only reasonable approach, especially when we are talking about an average of years, is to measure the surplus or deficit on a reserve-settlement basis. And, of course, the International Monetary Fund sets up the principle that international adjustments should take place at fixed parities—not fixed for all time, but adjustable under certain conditions.

Whether this system has worked well or not is a separate question. My own conclusion would be that, on the whole, it has worked very well—or at least worked well until 1964—and that the difficulties which have arisen since 1964 are attributable to defects in national policies and not to a basic fault in the system itself.

In discussing adjustment, let me first say a word about the sources of payments difficulties. We are all familiar with the fact that when a country has an inflation or an excessive boom, it is almost bound to run into a payments problem; and, as Fritz pointed out, if it keeps up the inflation for a long time, it will build into the structure of its economy an excessively high level of prices and costs relative to other countries. Thus the country can have a payments problem that continues after the excessive demand has been eliminated.

But there are other sources of payments problems. It is not unusual to find payments difficulties that arise, not from inflation, but from unfavorable changes in the world economic environment—changes that adversely affect a country's level of exports or imports. For example, the creation of the European Common Market, with its commercial preferences and discrimination, has resulted in a structural change affecting favorably the Common Market countries and affecting adversely the United Kingdom and the United States. One could easily cite other examples of unfavorable developments in what I would call the "real demand" or—to go back to John Stuart Mill—the "reciprocal demand" for exports and imports.

Under the Bretton Woods philosophy, a country that has a persistent deficit is not expected to adjust the balance of payments by deflating the economy. Of course, if the country is inflating, it should stop the inflation. But, as I have said, merely stopping the inflation may not restore balance even in cases where inflation is the culprit that produced the difficulty. If stopping the inflation doesn't correct the situation, or if the imbalance is caused by structural factors rather than by inflation, the Bretton Woods prescription is to change the exchange rate. Between 1949 (I start after the devaluations of that year) and 1964, there were several major changes in parity involving the developed countries, including two appreciations—those of the Netherlands and of Germany. Since 1964, however, the resistance to changes in parity has become great, notwithstanding some very serious maladjustments in international payments. Something has gone askew, and therefore I agree fully that we need to talk about improving the international adjustment process.

But how? To begin with, what is the responsibility of surplus countries? This is a question I first had the pleasure of discussing in 1943 in responding to the view of Lord Keynes that what we want is a system where adjustment takes place through expansion in the surplus countries, not through contraction in the deficit countries. I call this the "fish-oil theory." According to this theory, if Norway alone, for example, has a continuing deficit in its balance of payments, all other countries must expand domestic demand until they buy enough fish oil to restore the Norwegian balance of payments. If we accept such a principle in a system of fixed parities, the country with the greatest inflation would be setting the pace for monetary policy in the whole world.

But if we reject the fish-oil principle, what should the deficit countries do? The problem, as we have seen, is more complicated than stopping an inflation, though that is the best place to begin, if inflation is causing the deficit. However, a change in the exchange rate may be needed, and resistance to such a change may be strong. Thus we should consider whether the adjustable-peg system established at Bretton Woods is in need of alteration.

First, let me say that the people at Bretton Woods, some of whom are around this table, were not as dogmatic as outsiders might think. The question of wider exchange-rate margins did arise; in fact, the U.S. Treasury issued a paper—I guess I must have written it—which came to the conclusion that a wider band would be helpful, particularly if the width were not so great as to disturb money markets by creating expectations of too much fluctuation. The paper favored a considerably wider band than we have today. The Europeans, however, turned this down; they preferred a band which, in effect, is the equivalent of what the gold points would be if the United States really did sell and buy gold freely. But I think we have reached a stage where there could be nothing but benefit from discussing whether the Bretton Woods system of fixed parities is an effective way of running the international monetary system, or whether the time has come to modify the system—perhaps a lot, perhaps a little. At this point, I am not taking a position; I am simply stating what I think are the big issues before us.

Chairman THORP: We turn now to our other authority from the Bologna conference, Bob Triffin.

ROBERT TRIFFIN: Let me start with what seems to me the most frightening aspect of the present crisis—the effect of the persistent deficits of the United States and the United Kingdom on two major world problems. The first concerns the functioning of the international capital market, and the second relates to the functioning of the international monetary system.

With regard to the international capital market, what has happened in recent years is that the two major financial centers of the world, the United States and the United Kingdom, have practically ceased to contribute to economic development abroad by net transfers of goods and services. In the years immediately preceding the First World War, if we can believe somewhat doubtful statistics, the United Kingdom exported capital to the tune of about 10 percent—not 1 percent but 10 percent—of her gross national product. Coming down to only 1 percent of GNP today would mean that the two major financial centers should export annually about $10 billion of capital to the rest of the world. In 1968, the current-account surplus of the United States was about $900 million; the current-account deficit of Britain was about $900 million. Total: zero. At the same time, the two countries took in almost $6 billion of earnings on previous investments. Thus, two of the richest countries in the world are now drawing resources from, rather than contributing resources to, the rest of the world.

Yet, for various reasons, capital markets do not adjust overnight to such a total change of situation. The adjustment is particularly slow in the long-term capital market. Both the United States and the United Kingdom have continued in recent years to export large amounts of long-term capital, but since these could not be financed from traditional sources—that is, from current account surpluses or short-term capital inflows—they have been financed by a huge decline in net monetary reserves.

This brings me to my second topic, the impact of these events on the monetary system. For a time, the decline in the net reserves of the United States and the United Kingdom could take place without great strain, because other countries continued to accumulate sterling and dollar balances as reserves. But this is no longer true. To borrow from Professor Machlup, it is quite clear that we cannot *reform* the gold-exchange standard, because it is *dead.*

Under the gold-exchange system, the two traditional sources of reserve increases were (1) gold and (2) spontaneous accumulation of dollar and sterling reserves. This situation has drastically changed. From the end of 1964 through September 1968, the gross reserves of the world increased by $4.8 billion, but the two traditional sources declined by $7.8 billion—that is to say, gold declined by $2.3 billion while liquid dollar and sterling balances declined by $5.5 billion. Therefore, the overall increase of $4.8 billion had to be fed by an increase of $12.6 billion in what I would call "*negotiated* increases in credit reserves." Among these are the rescue agreements concluded in Basle repeatedly over the last few years, the transformation of liquid dollar holdings into nonliquid dollar holdings, and so on. There is no longer a gold-exchange standard; there is a *negotiated credit reserve standard,* or we might call it a mutual-bluff standard, based on the knowledge that Europeans can threaten the United States with pulling gold out of Fort Knox, while the United States can threaten Europeans with closing the doors to Fort Knox.

Now I come to the problem of what can be done—the question of reform in relation to international adjustment. Let me say first that what I miss in the SDR [Special Drawing Rights] agreements of September 1967 is any kind of link between reserve creation and international adjustment, in spite of all the attention given earlier to this matter by the Group of Ten. It was decided at Rio that the new reserves created in the form of SDR's would be distributed automatically to everybody, irrespective of the adjustment or maladjustment policies pursued by them. Moreover, Rio forgot to discuss the role of the traditional reserve assets—gold and the reserve currencies; it concentrated only on the new SDR's, and therefore one could foresee that the sterling, dollar, and gold crises would continue, since a serious problem had been swept under the rug.

In considering what can be done, I think that the first point to be stressed is that surplus countries should not retain the exorbitant privilege, which they enjoyed under the gold-exchange standard and which they continue to enjoy under the present system, of being able to decide for themselves exactly how their surpluses should be financed. If they want to be in surplus, they should not have the right to have the surplus settled in gold for amounts far in excess of current accretions of monetary gold in the world—that is to say, they should not have the right to raid the gold reserves of other countries and impose on them deflation, devaluation, or restrictions. Nor should they have the choice, which they have now, of deciding instead to finance their surpluses by accumulating either sterling or dollars, while retaining the privilege of changing their minds tomorrow and transforming their sterling into dollars, or their dollars into sterling, or both into gold. This is no longer a workable system, and therefore it calls for fundamental reform.

Finally, a few words on a subject which undoubtedly will occupy much of our time at this conference—the famous panacea of greater flexibility of exchange rates. In many ways, I agree that more flexibility in exchange rates is needed, but I don't think that such flexibility can be automatic, since payments problems may be due to three totally different causes, each calling for a different approach. First, there may be temporary deficits due, for example, to speculative movements. Applying a change in exchange rate to what is purely a temporary disequilibrium would simply distort the pattern of exchange rates in the future. A second source of deficits is what I would call overspending; a country spends more than its current real resources. The result is inflation and a payments deficit. If you try to cure that through readjustment of exchange rates, you may temporarily eliminate the deficit by exporting more and importing less, but at the cost of accelerating the domestic inflation, as there will be fewer goods available to meet the excess demand. Overspending can be cured only by cutting the spending and not by changing the exchange rate. There is finally the third case, in which the exchange-rate remedy is indeed appropriate: a distortion in the international price and cost pattern. But even in this case, simply permitting rates to be flexible would not automatically solve the problem. If the Germans in November 1968 did not accept the pressures put upon them by the United States, the United Kingdom, France, and other countries to let the mark go up, it is quite clear that saying "you can have flexibility" would not impose flexibility on the surplus countries. Any flexibility *imposed* by such a system would be exclusively on the deficit countries. When they lost their reserves, they would no longer be able to intervene in the market to maintain the exchange rate. The surplus countries, on the other hand, could always accumulate more reserves and thus impose the whole burden of exchange-rate adjustment on the deficit countries.

To deal with this problem, I would suggest, not a band system, but what I would call a "fork" or "prong" system. Under the prong system, each country would undertake to keep its exchange rate stable within limits determined by its reserve accumulations or its reserve losses. Thus a country would intervene in the market to keep its rate stable so long as its reserve losses—or its reserve accumulations—did not exceed a certain percentage, say 30 percent, of its normal reserves. Beyond this percentage, a country which was losing reserves would be required to consult with the Fund. But a surplus country would be exposed to the same kind of discipline. If it increased its reserves beyond the agreed percentage, it would have to discuss the situation with the Fund, and if no agreement could be reached on what should be done, the country would be enjoined from continuing to support its exchange rate by buying foreign exchange from the market. At that point, its rate would go up; that is, flexibility would be imposed on the surplus country, just as flexibility would be imposed on the deficit country when it lost the agreed percentage of reserves.

Let me say that Professor Machlup supports essentially the same view in many of his writings. This approach is not entirely new. In the European Payments Union Agreement, to which we might look for other constructive suggestions, you will remember that when a creditor country had accumulated surpluses in excess of its quota, it had no right automatically to get gold, dollars, or anything else from the deficit countries; the nature of future settlements had to be discussed and agreed upon by the entire EPU membership. In any case, the prong system that I have outlined would introduce flexibility of exchange rates where needed, and a country could jump rather than crawl if a jump were more appropriate. I think that this system would be the best way to introduce greater exchange-rate flexibility, without pretending to make it automatic or to apply it to problems which cannot be cured by that method.

CHAPTER III

DIALOGUE ON THE ISSUES

Chairman THORP: Having heard from those who have officially been given priority, we can now turn to those who speak because they really want to speak. Realizing that the college professors around this table are accustomed to talking fifty minutes at a time, the chairman is going to have to be quite impolite. I am going to allot each speaker five minutes, plus or minus a bit; after all, we don't want to stop a brilliant idea in the middle of a phrase.

At this stage, I am proposing an exchange of views on the key issues we should have in mind as we try to develop a national or an international approach to this problem of adjusting our various economies to each other—economies which in their domestic situation seem to march off in different directions. It has interested me that all three of our opening speakers have emphasized that our problem originates, to a large extent, from differences in national behavior. How do we deal with this difficulty? We do have a national program to promote adjustment, but I don't think there are many people who feel that it is sure to be successful or that is is the best that can be devised. Thus we are talking about an exceedingly real problem both for the United States and for the rest of the world.

A few conference members have already indicated to me that they would like to speak on this theme. I will reject the conventional use of the alphabet and start with Henry Wallich.

HENRY C. WALLICH: Mr. Chairman, I would like to speak on some neglected aspects of international adjustment. That makes me a very poor man to begin this dialogue, before speakers have neglected those aspects. But in the public discussion thus far, I think it is fair to say that the particular problems of the United States with the various proposals for a wider band, for a crawling peg, and for border taxes have not been properly brought out. The United States encounters certain difficulties that make all these devices less attractive than they seem in the abstract. As I look at these proposals, I find myself like the man with a dog who said that the more he saw of people, the better he liked his dog. The international monetary system is something of a dog, but it has worked since the war. It has been declared defunct for a long time; in fact, it has worked longer under the declaration of being defunct than it did before. We need to be sure that whatever replaces it is really better.

As for the band, the United States ties to gold, and other countries tie to the dollar. The United States, therefore, cannot have a band; it is subject to the kind of movements within a band that other countries initiate. If countries decide to depress their currencies within that band, the dollar is a sitting duck, in danger of losing its competitiveness. Of course, if we insist on nonintervention within the band, the true value of currencies will be reflected in the movement of each. But I do not see the possibility of nonintervention, because every action of monetary policy, via capital movements, automatically becomes an act of intervention. To that extent, the United States can also intervene. However, if our domestic monetary policy is then to be geared to trying to push out dollars or to bring in foreign currencies, it would not be a very attractive policy posture.

Much the same can be said of the crawling peg. It makes no sense for the United States to crawl against gold as long as others are pegged to the dollar; others will crawl against the United States. If others inject a downward bias into their crawl, as they quite possibly can, U.S. competitiveness again diminishes. If we envisage a realistic situation—that is, that by no means all countries avail themselves of these facilities, should they ever be instituted—then we probably will have blocs floating or crawling, and very likely there will be only two blocs. In that case, I think it would be very difficult to establish rules for either the width of the band or the rate of the crawl.

Take the third possible means of adjustment, border taxes. We do not even have indirect taxes to compensate for through an export subsidy. We might, nevertheless, move in this direction with the help of a GATT [General Agreement on Tariffs and Trade] waiver and an agreement not to retaliate. The border-tax device is the one way in which I can see a country like the United States getting from one fixed exchange rate to another. And that, I think, is what the world wants—not floating rates but changes in fixed rates, once it is decided that changes in rates are needed. But I do not agree with my good friend, Fritz Machlup, that there is a clear case for overvaluation of the dollar. We have a war, we have an inflation, and I think it is quite impossible to arrive at a judgment on that question.

Finally, a few words about the idea of a pure dollar system, with the dollar inconvertible into gold and other countries deciding whether to float, peg, or control. That arrangement would not really relieve the United States of the problems it faces under the present system. We would have a new set of constraints. If foreign countries were to peg to the dollar, we would be confronted with occasional crises as countries unpeg and move in one direction or the other. In trying to forestall those crises, we would find ourselves tempted to do much the same things we are compelled to do now. Basically, any system in which the United States lends its currency to the world as an intervention and reserve medium requires discipline on the part of the United States, regardless of whether the dollar floats in some sense or whether the dollar is pegged to by other countries.

In closing, I would like to stress the very great service the United States renders the world in making its currency available. If it were easy to replace the dollar as an international medium, surely the European Economic Community, which has engaged in ten years of thinking about the problem, would have found a way of doing it. But thus far the dollar has not been replaced, and nobody knows how it could be done.

WILLIAM R. ALLEN: It is heartening to have a conference directed to the theme of international adjustment. One would expect James Meade to say, as he did at the Bologna conference two years ago, that how countries "adjust their payments to each other" is a problem "much more important" than "the various ways of controlling and increasing international liquidity." It is perhaps more striking to find Edward Bernstein agreeing. At the same meeting, he said, "Clearly, the adjustment process is very important. In a sense, indeed, adjustment is the most important question, because the only reason for having a discussion on reserves is to make adjustment easier." Less surprisingly, he contended that "the adjustment process in the postwar world has worked reasonably well." But he revealed the nudity of the emperor by adding: "The United States and the United Kingdom are perhaps exceptions."

Some of us have long insisted that there simply is no adjustment mechanism under the IMF [International Monetary Fund] arrangement, and it follows from that conclusion that recurrent crisis is well nigh inevitable. Strain and occasional disaster have, indeed, been the continuing thread in the history of international finance since World War II. Most of the commercial world has operated—floundered, staggered, lurched, and improvised would be more descriptive verbs—under the IMF, and the proposition that the Fund must be deemed a success because the world economy in general has prospered is a non sequitur of truly monumental proportions.

When we talk of international adjustment, we are implying, of course, that there is an imbalance to adjust, a deficit or surplus to be corrected, a gap to be eliminated. Here we are in great shape in what is, in most respects, a vale of scarcity; we have a wealth of measuring sticks. There is Walther Lederer's "overall" balance; there is Bernstein's "official settlements" balance; there is the concept of "basic" balance. Of course, if one prefers the Economics of Joy, one can conclude, with Despres, Kindleberger, and Salant, that it is wholly right and proper for the United States to lend long and borrow short, and that our payments problem will disappear as this minority view becomes predominant.

Whatever our views on this matter may be, it does not seem necessary that, in our efforts to achieve balance (however defined), we take it upon ourselves to determine the equilibrium exchange rate and then peg it—and repeg it again and again as the equilibrium value changes over time and the spirit moves us to make these alterations. Exchange rates are prices, and prices which are free to fluctuate are equilibrium-inducing variables in the market. Therefore, it hardly seems heretical in a covey of economists to suggest that such variables should be allowed to vary. The most desirable variable rates should, by definition, be between "optimum" currency areas. I am at least psychologically prepared to negotiate on the question of what are—both conceptually and empirically—optimum currency areas. But I do not anticipate being persuaded that one such area subsumes the entire noncommunist world.

In conclusion, a major problem of internal external equilibrium is still with us. In one set of manifestations or another, it is bound to persist so long as we lack a genuine mechanism of international adjustment, and, as was conceded even by Lord Keynes, under the IMF arrangement there is no adjustment mechanism. What we require is not a discretionary and ad hoc type of policy to direct and decree market behavior but rather a design of institutions to induce behavior which yields internal and external equilibrium. And one promising feature of such a design is freely fluctuating exchange rates.

RICHARD N. GARDNER: I recently had occasion to look back at the Bretton Woods negotiations in an effort to draw an assessment twenty-five years later. I was struck that the founders of this system, or non-system as some of us would have it, were very clear that there were three main alternatives in international adjustment. There was adjustment through trade and exchange controls. They didn't want that, and I trust we don't want it. They saw that there was a possibility of adjustment through freely fluctuating exchange rates. They objected to that but favored a system of fixed parities with only occasional resort to exchange-rate adjustments. It is very interesting that they came down quite hard, in the original Keynes and White Plans, on the third type of adjustment—that is, the harmonization of domestic and international policy.

In the unpublished first draft of the White Plan, the members of the IMF were obliged "not to adopt any monetary or banking measure promoting either serious inflation or serious deflation without the consent of a majority of member votes of the Fund." When the plan was published, this far-reaching provision was omitted, but the Fund was authorized to make recommendations for changes in economic policy to countries having serious deficits or surpluses. These recommendations were reinforced by sanctions—the denial of the use of Fund resources beyond a certain point in the case of a deficit country and the rationing of a scarce currency in the case of a surplus country. And under the Keynes Plan, the Clearing Union could require a deficit country drawing over half its credit facilities to deposit collateral, depreciate its currency, or control outward capital movements. A surplus country whose credit balance exceeded half its quota could be required to stimulate domestic demand, appreciate its currency, reduce import barriers, or make international development loans.

I recall these recommendations because the framers of the system, at least initially, recognized that the third method of adjustment—conformity of domestic with international policy—was to be the central one. Unfortunately, in the negotiations before Bretton Woods and at Bretton Woods, this emphasis on adjusting national economic policies was pushed aside, partly because the British and ourselves could not agree on just who should bear the burden of adjustment—the surplus country or the deficit country—and partly because, with an eye on Congress and Parliament, it was thought better to leave out such explicit references to the modification of national economic sovereignty. But I suggest that, twenty-five years after Bretton Woods, we can no longer duck this tough issue. Our challenge is to find some ways of harmonizing more effectively these national economic policies.

We need to build into the national economic decision-making process, more adequately than we have in the past, consideration of the implications of international adjustment. This means more effective consultation. It may also mean some structural changes in our constitutions and in our administrative practices—for example, the delegation by our Congress, to the executive branch, of the power to alter tax rates within certain margins must be accomplished. We simply cannot continue to put up with the situation of waiting more than a year before a tax proposal is approved by the House Ways and Means Committee.

I would like to see the International Monetary Fund restored to its place of primacy in dealing with the adjustment problem, as was envisaged at Bretton Woods. We deal in episodic fashion with adjustment problems in the OECD [Organization for Economic Cooperation and Development] Working Party III, in the Basle Club, and in the Group of Ten, but the IMF is really rather ineffective in this area. Could we not consider constituting a Group of Twenty-One, to include representatives of the member countries on the IMF Executive Board, plus Switzerland, which would meet at the ministerial level every three months or so, to face these hard adjustment questions and, if necessary, to bear down on the countries having chronic surplus or deficit positions. I say Group of Twenty-One, because it seems to me anomalous, and not really right, that countries like India and Brazil should be excluded from a caucus that deals with the adjustment problem. They have a legitimate interest in how adjustments are made by the rich countries—whether through cutting aid, or reducing imports, or deflation. These are matters that affect all the countries of the world, less developed as well as developed, and I think the less developed countries have a right to participate.

Finally, we need to look again at the role of trade restrictions in the adjustment process. It is anomalous that, when GATT was founded, the most pernicious type of trade restriction—quantitative restriction—was the only type authorized to deal with balance-of-payments adjustment. Surely we ought to consider amending Article XII and other provisions of GATT to permit adjustment through import surcharges and export subsidies. I recognize that there may be risks in expanding the range of trade devices that countries can legitimately employ for adjustment purposes, but the fact is that these devices are being used, and they need to be subjected to safeguards and international supervision. There is an even stronger case for revising GATT to recognize the special obligations of surplus countries unilaterally to reduce tariffs and border taxes and to diminish rebates and other export incentives.

GOTTFRIED HABERLER: My friend, Richard Gardner, has raised a point that I would like to discuss. I have been struck, as I am sure many of you have, that inside a country the adjustment mechanism works somehow—we don't know exactly how, but it does work smoothly and efficiently—whereas internationally it does not work well. I have an answer to that riddle; the mechanism works internally because inside a country policies are harmonized. California cannot inflate while New York deflates; we have a Federal Reserve System which sees to it that, if there is inflation or deflation, it is going on everywhere at the same time. Of course, I recognize that there are other factors, but this is, in my opinion, the most important reason why internally the adjustment mechanism works, whereas externally it does not work.

Under the old gold standard, however, there was an international adjustment mechanism which did work to some extent. It worked because, at that time, countries put exchange stability foremost. They were not as much interested in full employment and growth as we are now. Moreover, at that time, wage rates were more flexible. At any rate, this is a thing of the past. We all want full employment, we all want rapid growth, and we have rigid wages. Therefore, my answer is that we cannot work a fixed exchange system. I think it is utopian, at least for the present, to believe that it is possible, as Dick Gardner hopes, to have an international harmonization of policies. I used to say that such harmonization may be possible in a small group, such as the European Common Market. The Common Market countries are homogeneous, equal to each other, and are in continuous consultation on all problems of policy. Even in this case, I must say, I was wrong. France has inflation, Germany has less inflation. If harmonization is not possible inside the Common Market, then I am sure it is not possible on an international level.

I agree with Professor Gardner that direct controls, especially quantitative controls, should be ruled out. We don't want them; they reduce the benefits which we all want from international division of labor. What is left? What about border taxes, as mentioned by Henry Wallich and Richard Gardner? Border taxes have been used recently by Germany and France, and Dr. Emminger in a recent speech quite rightly called them a bad substitute for changes in exchange rates—"Ersatz devaluation and appreciation."

Why are border taxes bad? They are never uniform. In the Common Market, where the Germans and the French have used them, agricultural products are excluded, services are excluded, and even after these exclusions the taxes are not uniform. And, of course, border taxes operate only on the import side. Well, you may say, let's add tax refunds for exporters; the Germans and the French in fact did that, but again it was not uniform. If the United States wanted to operate under such a system, it would have to set up an entirely new dimension of international economic policy, and we can be sure that the import taxes and export subsidies would not be across the board; there would be selections, and the result would be little better than exchange control.

It is possible, of course, to regard border taxes as a sort of "half depreciation," which may be followed a year or two later by the second half—namely, a full depreciation. But suppose you do that. After you have taken the first step, people will expect the second half. I think this invites speculation and, therefore, such a policy has to be excluded.

What remains? The only thing that remains is flexibility of the exchange rate, limited or unlimited. I realize, as Henry Wallich has pointed out, that flexibility is a complicated matter, especially limited flexibility. But I think these complications can be dealt with successfully, and I am very glad that the problem is now being studied seriously in the Fund and elsewhere.

Let me speculate for a moment on how the combination of a wider band and a crawling peg would have operated if the system had been in effect a year ago. The French franc at that time was strong; it would have been at the upper edge of the band. Then came May, the student rebellion, and inflation in France. The franc would have gone down to the lower limit of the band. If the margins on either side of parity had been 4 or 5 percent, the French would have automatically had a depreciation of 8 or 10 percent, and that would have relieved the situation. A year ago, the German mark perhaps would not have been at the upper limit of its band but, say, near the middle. During the year, it would have gone up, and this would have helped a good deal. Of course, you will say that inflation in France was so bad that the rate might stay at the lower limit of the band. That is true, but, with the crawling peg, the band itself would gradually move downward, either automatically or by discretion.

I do not say that a wider band and a sliding band are panaceas. I can imagine maladjustments in the balance of payments so serious that such measures would not be enough. But certainly, if this system had been in operation, we would not be worse off than we are now; and, looking back over the last fifteen years and at the changes in price levels that have taken place in all the industrial countries over that period, it is hard to avoid the conclusion that these changes could have been accommodated by a band of 4 percent on either side of parity and by a slide of not more than 2 percent a year. I am not sure that this will always be so, but the system certainly would reduce disequilibria and the need for imposing controls. Just let me remind you that France has full-fledged exchange control, as does Great Britain. We have not gone that far, but we are on the way. If we have another crisis and if we continue, as we have in the past, to impose one control after another, we shall be there soon.

ROBERT SOLOMON: I would endorse some, if not all, the "neglected" points to which Henry Wallich referred in his remarks, and, if I may, I will simply add two or three considerations.

First, we are focusing on the adjustment process and are not concerned primarily with liquidity or with the confidence problem, but I think that it is probably not possible to examine the adjustment process without taking into account the relationship between the liquidity problem and the adjustment problem. That is to say, adequate growth of liquidity may be a necessary condition for satisfactory adjustment. It is obviously not a sufficient condition, but it is probably a necessary condition, and therefore I think that the topic of liquidity has to be on the table from that point of view.

Second, in discussing international adjustment, we should devote some attention to the balance-of-payments aims of the various countries around the world. The desire of countries to increase their reserves is what relates the adjustment problem to the liquidity problem, but, apart from that, we need to examine the consistency of balance-of-payments objectives with respect to the current account. Professor Machlup, in his very interesting opening statement, pointed out that Germany has a current-account surplus of some $4 billion or $5 billion, which he believes Germany wishes to maintain, and he concluded that, if Germany has that big a current-account aim, it is ridiculous for the United States to have as small a current-account surplus as it has now. One can turn that around and say that not every country can have a current-account surplus; what we must ask ourselves is whether the payments objectives of the various countries—or at least the various areas—of the world are consistent, and, in particular, whether their current-account aims are consistent with their intentions concerning the flow of capital. This point seems to me relevant to our discussion of the techniques for international adjustment, whether they take the form of more flexible exchange rates, or border taxes, or other measures.

My third point is concerned with the willingness of countries to use adjustment techniques. We are obviously going to be talking this weekend about various exchange-rate flexibility devices. What do we do with the following problem? The European Economic Community has apparently integrated to such a degree that the member countries are highly reluctant to have their exchange rates fluctuate against each other, yet the Community has not integrated enough to be willing or able to move as a bloc. This is a behavior problem, an institutional problem, that I think we should discuss if our deliberations are to be realistic and fruitful.

ROBERT Z. ALIBER: As I look at this group of distinguished elder statesmen, I think it would be comparative advantage on my part to be seen and not heard, and therefore I will be brief.

My first point is that our adjustment choices ought to be congruent with what is happening in the world. We economists give much advice on what ought to be done about the liquidity problem. No one takes it; things turn out badly, but we pat ourselves on the back and conclude that, if only we could change sovereignty in the world, any of the various plans that have been offered would be workable. I suggest that we may have the problem backwards; what we need to do is to find an adjustment mechanism which is consistent with the locus of sovereignty.

I will mention only two points here. One is that, in most countries, the value attached to domestic objectives is clearly being given more and more weight than the value attached to international objectives. The second point is the increasing attention given to decentralized decision-making. I think that Dick Gardner ended up at the right railroad station when he spoke of this point, but unfortunately he got on the wrong train. In this world, I think both monetary and fiscal policy are really dead for international purposes; they are now designed almost exclusively for domestic purposes.

This observation brings me to the issue of how we get to exchange-rate flexibility. We are going to have greater exchange-rate flexibility. The question is simply where the market will meet the institutional mechanism—where the market will meet the monetary authorities.

We have a large number of choices. We could go to a system, as in the 1920's, of unfettered flexibility. We could go to a system, as in the 1930's, of managed intervention. We could go to a system, as in the 1940's and 1950's, of extensive controls and of exchange-rate flexibility through control devices. We could achieve flexibility through a tax-subsidy scheme. We should try to answer this question: Where, in our search for flexibility, should the market meet the institutional mechanism? I suggest this as the central focus of our deliberations.

C. FRED BERGSTEN: I would like to make my remarks on two planes—first, on the plane of pure economics and, second, on the plane of political economics. Let me start on the first plane and indicate what I see as our main options. In Washington, we talk a lot about options, and that is what I would like to do now.

I see three major options for changing the rules of the adjustment game. The first is the use of administrative controls. I am not citing that as an improvement, but simply as a major option which is being widely used now and which, barring some improvement in the system, will probably be used on a wider scale. Administrative controls range all the way from pervasive exchange controls that deal with every part of the external accounts to selective controls administered on specific parts of the trade or capital accounts.

The second option covers what are called "market-oriented" controls. Here, "controls" is not too good a word, but I have in mind such devices on the current account as border taxes and such devices on the capital account as the interest-equalization tax. The border tax has been discussed a good deal, and I only want to remind people that, when coupled with export subsidies, it can be regarded as a kind of partial exchange-rate change, limited generally to the trade account. My other example, the interest-equalization tax, places a wedge, so to speak, between the domestic interest-rate structure and the international interest-rate structure in order to free domestic monetary policy to some extent from external constraints. Market-oriented controls are an important option; they have been used a good deal, and their use is increasing.

The third major option, which has already received considerable attention around this table, is the greater use of exchange-rate changes. Here I would distinguish between two general approaches. One would be the approach Robert Triffin recommended, of trying to build into the system a better mechanism for assuring jumps in the peg when they are needed—in other words, for assuring more effective operation of the adjustable-peg system which Eddie Bernstein developed twenty-five years ago. It is tough to figure out how to do that, particularly in the light of Bob Solomon's reference to behavioral considerations, but this is one direction in which to move. The alternative is to go in the direction of greater flexibility of exchange rates, a subject on which much has already been said.

Let me now turn briefly to the plane of political economics. Here I want to focus on one problem—the persistent payments imbalance of the past ten years between the United States, on the one hand, and continental Western Europe, on the other. This has been the major continuing imbalance in the world. Is it a disequilibrium situation? Imbalance and disequilibrium may not mean the same thing, and I would agree with Fritz Machlup and others that even if we removed U. S. inflation from the picture—which is a big assumption—an imbalance would still remain. So my question is whether we are actually dealing with a disequilibrium situation or not. If we are not, then perhaps no adjustment is needed. But if we are, then we have to look at the various adjustment options I have just outlined.

The major adjustment device that the United States has used thus far is capital control, both of the administrative type and of the market-oriented variety. The result (though other causes have contributed) has been a decline in U.S. net capital exports. And that result, looked at from a European standpoint, may be less unhappy than the other options, since the reduced flow of American capital to Europe has a favorable political implication on the Continent. The alternative approaches would all involve an improvement in the U.S. current account and, for that reason, would surely be less popular with the Europeans. Of course, a strong U.S. current-account position, matched by a large capital outflow to the less developed countries, would not be a problem; we would all be happy, including the Europeans. But we know that the bulk of any increased U. S. capital outflow would, in fact, go to the developed countries—to Western Europe,

Japan, Australia, and Canada, all of which have in some degree a political problem regarding capital coming from the United States. So in political terms, capital restraints by the United States may be the least unsatisfactory among the various adjustment options.

When we look at the other options, we come to the points made by Henry Wallich. As he said, in considering the possibility of greater exchange-rate flexibility, we must face the fact that the special role of the dollar does mean that the United States cannot get as much adjustment by this route as can other countries. So long as the dollar remains the center of the international monetary system, the United States is highly circumscribed in taking action in the exchange-rate field. This is not true of the border-tax approach, under which the United States could take initiatives and could get effects equal to those of other countries, because the special role of the dollar would not be involved. I am not saying that I advocate either of these options, but I hope that I have said enough to reveal some tough economic and political questions—questions which we need to grapple with if we are going to probe deeply into adjustment issues.

GARDNER PATTERSON: Several members have already noted that, in examining adjustment issues, we need to look at a much wider range of subjects than the purely monetary ones, and I would like to support what Mr. Bergsten has just said by expressing my hope that this group will spend a bit of time on the role in adjustment of variations in trade restrictions. I think that failure to grapple with this problem simply means that we are giving up a chance to try to improve what, in fact, governments are going to do.

Trade restrictions of various kinds are going to be used, not only because they may be the line of least resistance politically, but because they do have something to be said for themselves. First, they're fast—some of them. Second, they are really less costly than some of the alternatives, which may entail costs that countries are not willing to bear. As compared with fluctuating exchange rates, they are less likely to be self-defeating, because they can be highly selective. I would certainly not want to suggest that variations in trade restrictions should be the sole or major technique on which a country should rely in seeking adjustment, but I think they have a place in a policy mix.

Of course there are problems. Where do surplus countries fit into the picture? How do we prevent restrictions that were introduced for payments reasons from staying on for protectionist reasons? I hope that we do find time to consider what might be done to minimize the evil effects of this approach, to specify the conditions under which variations in trade restrictions clearly would not be appropriate, and also to discuss the conditions under which trade restriction may be only the second-best or third-best choice, but still the best that is politically available.

This approach, I would emphasize, has a positive as well as a negative side. Surely, one of the most interesting things about the European Payments Union was that differential rates of trade liberalization—that is to say, differential rates in the removal of trade restrictions—played a prominent role in the adjustment process. And the proposal that was made a year or so ago to change the timing of the Kennedy Round tariff cuts, speeding up some and slowing down others, seems to me a promising way of dealing with some of our present adjustment difficulties.

SIR ROY HARROD: International adjustment is a perplexing matter. There are two kinds of cases—simple cases and what Dr. Emminger calls conflict cases. In the simple cases, either domestic unemployment is combined with an external surplus or overfull domestic demand is combined with an external deficit. In the former case, inflate; in the latter, deflate. The conflict cases occur when excess domestic demand is accompanied by an external surplus, or domestic unemployment by an external deficit. My observations, extending over many years now, have been that the conflict cases are just as frequent as the simple cases.

I submit that deflation should be ruled out in cases where it would cause unemployment. I regard the deliberate creation of unemployment as immoral. Unemployment is a very terrible thing. If it is objected that we sometimes have to do terrible things to achieve greater good, the answer is that in this case there are other ways of getting that greater good.

Unfortunately, it is not possible to be very simple about these other ways. Of prime importance would be an "incomes," or "guide-posts," policy, whether voluntary or mandatory. We know that great difficulties attend an incomes policy. If only it could be achieved, I would prefer it to devaluation in its various forms, because the latter means the surrender of one objective by the devaluing country—namely, stable domestic prices—whereas an incomes policy does not.

Both incomes policy and devaluation depend, as we all know, on demand elasticities being sufficiently great. It is sometimes said that, if devaluation fails to improve a balance, an upward valuation *must.* But it occurs to me that there may often be a Hall-Hitch kinked demand curve at the existing parity.

I should like to note in passing my view that a freely floating exchange rate would produce intolerable oscillations, while a managed flexible rate, or a crawling peg, whether managed or automatic, would require larger reserves than a fixed exchange rate. The whole business of the exchange-rate recipe is rather dicey. This being so, I submit that trade restrictions should be regarded as legitimate for a deficit country. I submit that the *marginal* benefits of the international division of labor are much smaller than the losses due to deflation when that curbs natural growth. There seems to be an almost religious taboo against even mentioning this mode of adjustment, which appeals so strongly to common sense. I hold that economists should ignore this taboo, and I am happy to note that Professor Patterson has just done so.

Finally, a few words on the specific challenge made to me and Dr. Heilperin about gold. I favor raising the price of gold, perhaps doubling it. I regard this as something ready to hand—not as a perfect solution, not as a solution for all time. People, ask me, "Why do you want to have gold dug out of the ground? Surely we're intelligent enough to print the right number of bits of paper." Of course we are, in principle, but I think we're not ready yet. I feel convinced that the very simple explanation for our recurrent crises is the right one—namely, that world reserves, in relation to world imports, are now less than a third of what we were working with before the war. It seems so obvious; we cut world reserves to less than a third, and how can we expect not to have all sorts of headaches, crises, and frustration?

If we could solve the problem by paper—if we could print enough paper to restore reserves to something like the prewar level—O.K. by me, but we can't do it. It isn't simply that the bankers would never agree. They're probably right in thinking that we couldn't print such a vast mass of paper while retaining confidence in that paper. We may one day be able to do it, but we can't suddenly jump to a position of an adequate amount of paper—because there is not the confidence. So we have this really very meager proposal to create Special Drawing Rights. It doesn't take us very far. And also, I must confess—I hope I'm not offending anybody—that I have come to distrust the inherent deflationary mentality of central bankers. I believe that gold, if it were put back into its place, would be a far more liberal taskmaster than the central bankers are likely to be in the next ten or twenty years. These are my reason for wanting to double the price of gold.

How might the change in price come about? We are told by Professor Machlup and others that the President can't raise the price of gold. My feeling is that the change would come like this. If the U.S. deficit were to continue at such a rate as to result in another serious international crisis, the United States might come to the point where it no longer pays gold. Then the ball would lie with the other central banks. For the time being, the price of gold would cease to have two tiers; there would be one floating price, and I think the leading central banks outside the United States would get together, work out an agreement, and peg the price at a new level. It would be very tiresome for central banks with large gold reserves to have this price bobbing up and down; they would peg it at what they judged a reasonable rate. The United States meanwhile would be isolated. Then, though Congress would not be ready to pass new legislation, perhaps for a long time, there would be a sort of ad hoc executive permission to sell gold above the $35 price. After all, the United States has a nice big pile of gold; it would hardly make sense to stop using it or to sell it at the present official price when everyone is prepared to give 50 or 100 percent more for it. My guess is that, de facto, the United States would soon be operating at the higher price, and then, for many years, there might be Congressional hearings with the result that finally, after a couple of decades, Congress would change the official price of gold. The timing wouldn't matter so long as the United States was already de facto in the system.

FRANK A. SOUTHARD, JR.: What I have to say is, in part, my reaction to some of the statements that I listened to with great interest and pleasure this morning. Of course, the fact that I was interested and had some pleasure doesn't necessarily mean that I agree with everything that was said. For one thing, I think it must be recognized that there have been numerous changes of parity and numerous examples of fluctuating rates, and that it is not at all accurate to say that the Bretton Woods movable-par system has not worked. It is true—and it may be a conspicuous flaw in the Fund Articles—that the Fund was given no overt legal power to agree with countries on a limited period in which they need not have a par value, but the Fund has encountered no difficulty at all in working out fluctuating-rate arrangements extra-legally or even in allowing its resources to be used to support such arrangements.

At the same time, it must be agreed that par-value changes are difficult; if they weren't difficult, we wouldn't be sitting around this table discussing this particular subject. Moreover, it is quite clear that countries do strive for exchange-rate stability. Once upon a time—in the early 1950's, I think—we said in the Fund annual report that most countries most of the time want stable fixed rates of exchange, and that is certainly the lesson of experience.

I believe we should also recognize that it is very difficult for countries to operate anything like a true fluctuating rate. Indeed, in the experience of the Fund, it is the hardest thing in the world to get a country to have a genuinely fluctuating rate of exchange; even when the monetary authorities say to us on a Monday morning that they'll have one, by Friday night the rate has stopped fluctuating. The propensity to peg rates is a propensity which none of us should ignore. It arises in considerable part because, whether we like it or not, the exchange rate is an important element in the whole policy panoply of a country. A Japanese official told me a couple of weeks ago that, so far as Japan is concerned, the par value of 360 yen to the dollar is the absolute center of the national policy framework, and that if the Japanese could not maintain that par, they would have no success at all with their Diet in getting acceptance of the line of policy which from time to time they have to carry out. The one thing they could not tolerate was any tampering with the par-value system.

In this connection, it is important not to focus on exchange-rate problems exclusively from the standpoint of a few countries, such as the Group of Ten. The Fund has 111 members and, even if one may think most of them are not important, *they* think they're important. And they have problems that by and large are not, in their view, solved by rate fluctuation or rate instability.

Having said that, I would like to comment very briefly on some of the points that have been discussed. I came here hoping to hear a good deal of discussion on wider spreads and crawling pegs. I have some real doubts about the efficacy and usefulness of either of those techniques, but I would like to hear more discussion about them. I was much interested in Bob Triffin's suggestion of what he called a prong system. Some of us have been thinking in recent weeks along the lines that Bob seems to be thinking, since we see real difficulties in a crawling peg system based on a formula which is in any way mandatory on all countries. We have been exploring the possibility of a second regime, alongside the par-value regime, which would be optional, but if a country opted for the new system, it would be subject to a set of criteria, including Bob's criterion of reserve loss or gain, which under given rules might trigger a mandatory examination of the country's situation. This could lead perhaps to very small changes in par values, or it could lead to larger ones; that would be something to be determined. But such a system, I am inclined to think, would be less erratic and produce less unwanted results than the crawling peg. In this connection, we might reflect on the fact that if we now had in operation a formula for a crawling peg based on market deviations from par, the last four months would have called for a devaluation of the German mark—a devaluation which I wouldn't have supposed anyone would have thought was very sensible.

Dick Gardner made a comment with which I very much agree, as I understand it. He said that we ought to try to grope our way to some improvement in the decision-making process which would give a proper role to the non-Ten—to the excluded 100 or so countries, big ones and little ones alike. In the Fund, we have worried a great deal about this matter. Nobody can admire the Bonn conference as an example of decision-making, and certainly this way of deciding policy is bitterly resented by the countries that are left out—and they include some quite "important" countries, if you will, like Australia and India.

To turn to other subjects, I was surprised to hear Professor Allen say that there is no effective adjustment process under the IMF and to hear Professor Aliber say that monetary and fiscal policy is dead so far as the international scene is concerned. I could not agree with either of these propositions. There have been numerous recent examples of smoothly working, effective adjustment. Japan I've mentioned; I could mention others like Mexico, Colombia, and Indonesia in the last year. In all these cases, fiscal and monetary policy has been an extremely important, indeed an indispensable, part of the adjustment process.

On the subject of Special Drawing Rights, I agree that the SDR can evolve in the direction Bob Triffin has advocated for a long time. But I feel that this is something we should decide after we get things started. It would be suicidal today to talk about the brave new deeds we could do with SDR's when we haven't yet obtained the first activation. I have no doubt that we will get ratification and activation, but I wouldn't want to forecast the date in either case.

Bob Solomon and I were remarking to each other on the plane coming out here that the last Council of Economic Advisers, in one of its reports, shocked some conservative people by making suggestions which implied that we could have a $4 billion issue of SDR's. Yet we find people—quite serious and sober people like Sir Roy Harrod—saying that it ought not to be difficult at all to have a $40 billion increase in liquidity through an increase in the price of gold. I suspect that it will be a brave world that will agree on, let's say, $3 billion of SDR's a year. Maybe we will learn how to use them and be a little bolder later. But I am expressing some incredulity that the world will deliberately add $40 billion to liquidity through a gold price increase when it will find the greatest difficulty in agreeing deliberately to add $4 billion.

PAUL A. SAMUELSON: The historic gold standard was premised upon a flexibility of internal price levels, so that there was an adjustment mechanism. In the modern mixed-economy world, I think that no one can rely upon the old deflate-if-the-gold-standard-tells-you-to-deflate psychology (or inflate whatever's necessary if it tells you to inflate). I agree with Mr. Aliber that domestic goals are becoming more important, but I would emphasize something just as significant—that we are not masters of our own house domestically. It isn't that we have domestic goals and achieve them at the expense of international equilibrium, but rather that we have wage-price spirals which are out of our control and which run counter both to our domestic goals and to international equilibrium.

Therefore, there is need for some kind of flexibility. We would all love to have stable exchange rates with equilibrium, but it isn't a choice that's available to us, and so the problem is whether we will have various capital controls, whether we will have market-oriented or direct trade controls, or whether we will have a measure of exchange-rate flexibility.

I assert that Bretton Woods had in it a fatal flaw. The mathematical structure on which it was based was incorrect. What it assumed was that a set of exchange rates which would work at one period of time would be the appropriate set at another period of time. I realize that there were avenues within Bretton Woods for changing from one quantum position to another, but one of our main problems is precisely the pain that is involved when the world knows that you're in the wrong root of the equations and before Bretton Woods gives the word to leap to the new root. In these matters, "if 'twere to be done, it were well it were done quickly" should be amended to read "'twere well it be done yesterday."

Now our problem of political economy is that the powers that be in the world—the men of affairs, the central bankers, the finance ministers—do not know how to get us to flexibility. I saw a book advertised with the title, *You Can't Get There from Here*; we don't know how to get to some measure of exchange-rate flexibility from the present position. But we can ask ourselves: Suppose we *did* achieve flexibility and had a conference like this after a decade or two; who would dream of wanting to go back to the present arrangement?

So as not to disturb the central bankers, I will not talk about floating exchange rates—that, as Oscar Wilde would say, would be much too shocking—but will talk instead about the crawling peg. Widening the band around a parity will not solve the problem if you're in the wrong equilibrium configuration, or if you're in disequilibrium, because you will immediately go to one of the limits, but widening the band in an equilibrium situation will actually economize on reserves. I would not agree, without much more research and thinking, with Sir Roy Harrod's assertion that a crawling peg, with a widened band around it, will require larger reserves than the present inflexible exchange rates. I think there would be a smaller need for reserves—with the proviso, which someone should analyze, that when it is clear in which direction for the next ten years the peg will crawl, there may be destabilizing substitution effects.

The biggest part of our subject has hardly been discussed here—namely, that our problem is a dollar problem. The American dollar for a long time was grossly undervalued, but for a long period since, alas, it has been grossly overvalued. The dollar is traveling and living upon its former undervalued status, but that status is decaying in the memory of everyone. Nobody now acts as if he really believed in the Kindleberger-Salant-Despres thesis that the dollar is better than gold or is as good as gold. There *was* a time when it was better than gold, because the next move for the dollar was persistently in a favorable direction, but the next move for the dollar now, in the opinion of all the people whose opinions matter, is down, not up.

Now I turn to my final remark, which comes from the field of economic theory. I don't think that the only reason for a system of fixed exchange rates getting out of kilter is that countries pursue differential macroeconomic policies. I was glad to hear Dr. Bernstein speak of Mill's reciprocal demand; I will add Taussig's name in this connection. There are substantive changes in the pattern of international trade which, aside from any misbehavior of the central bank or of the fiscal authorities, call for changes in exchange rates. Now, in the past, changes in price levels might be a substitute for that, but my first axiom is that we can no longer rely upon those price-level changes. And we live in a world in which international equilibrium can be disturbed by things like a heating up of the Cold War, like the European miracle of productivity, like the discovery that American know-how can be utilized with European labor and that American laborers are not six feet seven and continental laborers five feet three. In such a world, it could be very helpful, in an orderly way, to change our exchange rates, just as with daylight-saving time, in an orderly way, we all change our watches.

Flexibility is not a panacea. If a country like Pakistan insists upon having real wages, let's say, of $4 an hour, there is no sliding-scale arrangement or floating rate which will yield Pakistan a $4 real wage. There are many things a country can do that are incompatible, and no change of the clock, no exchange-rate gimmick can make them compatible; but there are also problems which can be solved, and solved in the short run, by exchange-rate flexibility. With a crawling peg, there would still be a need for escape valves, because if we are too much out of equilibrium, we will have to move by a jump, or by a prong device, to another level of the peg. But that problem exists in even greater degree under the present system.

MICHAEL A. HEILPERIN: I would like to start by expressing my very deep satisfaction with the subject of this conference. For ten or fifteen years, we have been discussing the problem of international liquidity. I have thought, for upward of thirty years, that the basic problem faced by the international monetary system is the problem of re-equilibrium in balances of payments, or of adjustment, and in my more recent writings, I have occasionally referred to the problem of liquidity as being Problem Number Two. We don't know how much liquidity we need unless we know how quickly we can adjust balances of payments to equilibrium positions. Special Drawing Rights may be good, bad, or indifferent—I don't really think they can be bad; they can be good or indifferent—but in any event their adoption is useful, because, for some time to come, there will be no need to discuss liquidity on an official level, so it will be possible to discuss the important thing, namely adjustment.

When we speak of adjustment, I think it would be well to bear in mind something that has not been mentioned—that there are only two categories of countries which have been able successfully to resist adjustment. The first are surplus countries—nobody can do very much about them under present arrangements—and the second are very large deficit countries, especially if they happen to be reserve-currency countries, because they can simply chalk off part or all of their deficit to the world, send out I.O.U.'s to their creditors, and go merrily onward with deficits and inflation.

These resistances to adjustment occur in a world which for

many years has not had an international monetary system, or at least not a complete one. I don't think we have had a complete monetary system since the breakdown of the international gold standard in 1914. It broke down, you remember, not because of its inner weakness, for it was still an expanding system then, but because of the First World War. In the 1920's and 1930's, we hardly restored the gold standard, but we did achieve the establishment of the gold-exchange standard, an arrangement praised by the Genoa conference of 1922. With the international financial crisis of 1931, that system became thoroughly discredited, yet we slipped right back into it after World War II. Ironically, the earlier gold standard was a very successful system, even though now it is considered as discredited by practically everybody. Of such paradoxes history is made.

I would suggest that some time should be devoted in our discussions to the functioning of the gold standard. It was a system under which we had, as under no other, a completely symmetrical relationship between the behavior of deficit countries and the behavior of surplus countries—not only symmetrical but simultaneous, the deficit countries correcting their deficits while the surplus countries were correcting their surpluses. This of course made adjustment much easier. And both deficits and surpluses were corrected promptly, which means that we could get along with much lower reserves than we now think necessary.

We have heard of numerous varieties—57, maybe—of fluctuating exchange rates, crawling pegs, galloping pegs, jumping parities, and all that kind of thing, but there is a basic tendency of governments, of central banks, and of the business community toward fixed parities. At the present time, the majority of academic opinion is completely at war with the people who run the economic life of the world. That, I think, should be recognized, and generally—at least in Academia—it is not.

Adjustment, if carried out promptly, need not result in the kind of unemployment Sir Roy Harrod has in mind. And I don't think it needs to result in deflation or inflation; it just needs a certain amount of international cooperation and a certain amount of synchronization of national policies. In a nationalistic world, such cooperation and synchronization are difficult to achieve, but in a nationalistic world everything is difficult to achieve except an international economic crisis, which of course is very easy to get into. We have been on the verge of an international monetary crisis for more years than we care to think of—certainly since 1960. The present system is a thoroughly unsatisfactory one, and I can find only one argument which would give it support. That argument is well stated in the last line of the first epistle of Alexander Pope's immortal *Essay on Man*: "One truth is clear, WHATEVER IS, IS RIGHT." That, I think, is the one basis for justifying the present arrangements. I don't believe they are acceptable by any other reasoning.

LLOYD A. METZLER: I did not attend the conference at Bologna, but I did meet with a group of Treasury consultants from 1960 to 1966. At the Treasury, I proposed a system of outright flexible exchange rates, with no government intervention whatsoever. I must say I was rather surprised that in this group of experts I was a minority of one. I don't mean that I was surprised to be in that kind of situation; in my position as professor of economics at the University of Chicago, I have been the only Democrat in a group of Republicans, but what did surprise me was to find myself a minority of one in a group of Democrats.

From what has been said thus far, it seems we are all agreed that almost every country is devoted to some kind of program to stabilize the level of prices and to promote full employment and a healthy rate of growth. But if we are devoted to these objectives, there is no alternative, in my opinion, to a system of flexible exchange rates. And in listening to this discussion, I am happy to see that, in contrast to the situation at the Treasury a few years ago, a considerable number of us are now on the side of the angels.

Chairman THORP: One of the unexpected statistical results that seems to be coming out of this conference is the number of people who describe themselves as being on the side of the angels. However, it is quite clear from the discussion that angels disagree, and heaven may be more interesting than we thought. Next is Walter Salant.

WALTER S. SALANT: I'm sorry you didn't call on me before saying that, because I was also going to plead that I was on the side of the angels and that there seemed to be several tribes.

We've had a good deal of discussion about the best ways

of making international adjustments and considerable expression of sentiment to the effect that, in switching our attention from the liquidity problem to the adjustment problem, we have come to grips with the more basic and the more important issue. My first point is that the distinction between these two problems is far from clear and that the assumption that we're in a terrible situation with regard to handling the adjustment problem *may* be a great exaggeration. At least we ought to look at that possiblity.

There is a great tendency to assume that the mere presence of a payments deficit or a payments surplus is an indication of a disequilibrium and a situation calling for adjustment. I would maintain, on the contrary, that deficits and surpluses are not good signals; they simply are not reliable indicators that there is a disequilibrium or that an adjustment is needed.

The propositions that I am going to make appear at various points in the literature, most of which has been written by the people around this table, but the points are apparently forgotten when we come to examine particular situations. My first proposition is that the presence of a surplus or a deficit is a poor signal when no allowance is made for the needed trend growth in net reserves. The implication of a need for a gradual growth of reserves is that the countries needing the increments of reserves have to have surpluses. This implies that a country having a surplus smaller than the appropriate growth of reserves requires, not a movement toward balance, but a still bigger surplus. In such a case, the presence of a surplus would give an entirely wrong indication that the country should take measures to reduce that surplus.

This relationship between the surplus and deficit positions of all countries taken together and the growth of net world monetary reserves leads to the question of what payments situations typically look like when the growth of reserves is inadequate. Early last year, after the sterling devaluation of late 1967, we saw what kind of payments situation arises when net reserves are leaking out of the system. Under such conditions, most countries may find themselves in deficit and, on the conventional signal, should take measures to get into balance. But the deficits of late 1967 and early 1968 did not indicate a disequilibrium in the relationship of countries to each other—or, at any rate, they did not indicate that alone—and a signal which is interpreted as meaning that the deficit country needs to take steps to get back into equilibrium with other countries is a totally misleading signal.

When net reserves are leaking out of the system, the relationship of all countries taken together is out of equilibrium with the stock and growth of net reserves. The assumption that the deficits call for adjustment of countries with each other is then seen to be an absurdity. This would be obvious if every country were in deficit, as conceivably could be the case. But the same general situation may occur in a less extreme form when net reserves are not actually leaking out of the system but are simply not increasing at a sufficiently rapid rate. Analytically, the situation is the same, and here too the presence of a deficit can be a misleading signal.

We get a wrong signal also when a country is a financial center and a reserve-currency country. For such a country, a deficit—even on an official-settlements definition—may not indicate a disequilibrium or a need to improve the payments position. There would be no disequilibrium and no need to take action if the increase in the country's liabilities to foreign monetary authorities were no greater than the desire of foreign monetary authorities to increase their holdings of the country's currency. In this situation, the reserve-currency country might have a substantial deficit, even on an official-settlements basis, but there would be no disequilibrium.

In this connection, Paul Samuelson expressed the opinion that everybody thinks the dollar is overvalued. He qualified his statement by saying, everybody "whose opinions matter"—in other words, everybody who counts. Well, I would say that the people who are buying and selling dollars should be included among those who count; in fact, one might ask, who else does? And, as we all know, private residents abroad, almost without interruption, have been increasing their holdings of dollars year after year. Why, then, should we accept the conclusion that the dollar is overvalued? It seems clear to me that a good deal of what has been regarded as a failure of adjustment is, in fact, either the reserve problem in disguise—that is, inadequate increments of reserves—or a failure to appreciate the role of reserve-currency countries. So what I would like to ask is: How big is the *real* adjustment problem—not how big is what seems to be, but may not be, the adjustment problem?

LEONARD S. SILK: I believe that the basic problem around

this table—as is inevitable when economists meet—is that the emphasis is primarily on the technical side of adjustment rather than on the political side. In terms of good economic theory, there are many ways to solve the adjustment problem. The problem can be solved with a fixed exchange-rate system; it can be solved with a flexible or a completely floating-rate system. One has many counters to play in the adjustment process, including all sorts of policy mixes, and it occurs to me that it may be futile to look for an optimal solution, just as there is no optimal game of chess. Out of a virtual infinity of options, there are selected moves one can make, given certain actions and responses from the other side of the chessboard.

Similarly with the game of international adjustment. There may be many good solutions. In any case, the adjustment problem does not plague us because of a lack of good technical solutions. It plagues us because it involves conflicts of nations—because it involves issues that divide countries in terms of, for example, how they regard gold. South Africa's interest in a higher gold price does not rest on grounds of economic theory, nor does France's interest in downgrading the role of the dollar. Accordingly, I think that more effort needs to be directed to the underlying politics of adjustment and perhaps a little less effort to proving, via economic theory, that one particular approach is superior to another approach.

ALVIN H. HANSEN: I have increasingly become convinced that the next forward step in international adjustment ought to be in the direction of greater flexibility of exchange rates. I feel this much more strongly than I did some years ago. I heartily endorse Professor Haberler's recent suggestion that the United States should encourage, not discourage, any country that is contemplating the introduction of flexibility, and I have become increasingly persuaded that the international monetary situation would have stood on firmer ground today if the British Labor Party had put the United Kingdom on a managed flexible exchange system immediately upon assuming office, instead of playing the off-and-on game of now expansion, now deflation.

How do we get to a system of flexible exchange rates? This is a question about which we should have some discussion.

Must we wait until there is a collapse, a complete breakdown of the system, or is there an easier route toward flexibility? I don't know whether there is an easier route, but the question clearly needs examination. With respect to our country, how could we move toward a flexible rate? The President, I suggest, might again do as President Kennedy did in 1961. Immediately after he assumed office, he announced that the United States would be prepared to redeem all official holdings of dollars in gold right down to the last ounce, and he quoted Chairman Martin of the Federal Reserve System as assuring that the law gave the President the power to do what he said he was prepared to do. And I think we should further state openly that, if and when our gold is gone, we would then go on a managed flexible exchange rate.

I still lean toward a bit of conservatism here in that I say *managed* flexible rate, because a managed rate seems to me preferable to a completely floating rate. Actually, the world has had a good deal of experience with flexibility; it is just not true that we know nothing about these things. Both big and small countries, including Great Britain and Canada, have been on flexible exchange rates for long periods of time.

To assure that flexibility would yield the fullest possible measure of support in expanding world trade, we should proceed at once to undertake a progressive removal of controls and restrictions on trade and capital movements. Such a policy would probably hasten the day when our gold reserves are all gone, though I'm not sure about that, because I wonder if the gold-hungry countries really want to hold all the world's monetary gold, which would give them no income at all. I am not at all sure they are that foolish, but if they are, if we lose all our gold, I would say: O.K., no matter, the sooner we adopt a flexible exchange-rate system, the better.

ARTHUR I. BLOOMFIELD: I have just a few disjointed remarks to make on the adjustment mechanism. Some of the points I had planned to make have already been anticipated, so I hope I can make these appropriately brief.

The first is a purely semantic point, and perhaps of no great importance. There seems to be a tendency more and more to regard the only kind of adjustment that counts—the so-called real adjustment—as adjustment of the balance on current account, and to regard any market-oriented measures to influence the flow of capital as not genuine adjustment but simply palliatives or means of induced financing. I wonder how Keynes would have regarded this attitude. I think of the famous remark he made in 1929 that, historically, the capital account has adjusted to the current account, rather than the other way around. It may be rather arbitrary to say that the only kind of adjustment that matters is that affecting the current account.

My second point is that I share Sir Roy's view that an incomes policy, if it could be effectively implemented, would be a very acceptable means of promoting adjustment by bringing about appropriate changes in relative prices at home and abroad. However, even if incomes policies could be effectively implemented in deficit countries, at best they could keep the price level stable, so that their effectiveness as an instrument for payments adjustment would still depend on some price rises in the surplus countries.

Another point made this morning concerns the potentialities of closer international cooperation and consultation on the adjustment mechanism. Quite a good deal has been accomplished by this channel with regard to international liquidity, but comparatively little has been accomplished thus far with regard to adjustment. I don't think we should have any illusions as to the extent to which international cooperation and consultation can bring about an improvement in the adjustment process. Certainly, one key problem that remains unsettled is the apportionment of responsibility for adjustment between deficit and surplus countries. So far, we have had a lot of noble statements on this matter, but I think that, for the most part, they are rather devoid of genuine meaning.

I would hope that wider acceptance and greater effectiveness of incomes policies, increased flexibility of budgetary policy, perhaps even development of new policy variables, could enable countries to achieve more effective reconciliation of their domestic goals with their balance-of-payments objectives under the present exchange-rate system. I would also hope that we would devise more effective and economically efficient means, other than direct controls, of influencing the flow of capital in appropriate directions. But I agree with Professor Hansen and others that, after all is said and done, we cannot escape the fact that, if we are to avoid continued proliferation of direct controls over the balance of payments, we will need more exchange rate flexibility, unless we are prepared to lower our priorities for domestic goals—and, frankly, I don't think we should.

If we move toward greater exchange-rate flexibility, I would hope that we could remain within the framework of the adjustable-peg system, with the proviso that there be international consultation—such as we had during the last two exchange crises—to avoid excessive devaluation and to minimize the risk of competitive devaluation. There would also remain a continuing need for large credits to permit exchange adjustments to be put through effectively without a disorganization of the exchange-rate system. I hasten to say that I am not at all unsympathetic to the wider band proposal, and I don't see why it could not be combined with the adjustable peg. I have less enthusiasm for the sliding parity.

P. T. ELLSWORTH: Eddie Bernstein raised the question, is the Bretton Woods system a good system? In response, I would say, for whom? The adjustable peg, which is the heart of the Bretton Woods adjustment system, is simply not open to the United States. If we were to try to devalue unilaterally, it wouldn't be allowed to happen; others would fasten their currencies to the dollar and not permit us to depreciate. To me, this implies what some have asserted—that the world is essentially on a dollar standard. It also suggests a possible solution for the United States, which is to ignore our balance-of-payments problems, remove the controls, and attend to the policies that are of primary importance to us. Incidentally, I am sorry to hear the controls referred to as adjustment mechanisms; to me, they are simply depressants of a deficit and not adjustments at all.

If the world, or a good share of the world, were to go on a dollar standard overtly, what would the continuance of the Bretton Woods system mean then? Well, it would be open to other countries either to peg to the dollar and accept increases in dollar deposits if we ran a deficit against them, or to change their parities. The objection to the continuance of the Bretton Woods system is that any adjustable-peg system inevitably means disequilibrium in the exchange rate because of the accumulation over time either of overvaluation or undervaluation of a currency. For this reason, I am led to join the good guys rather than the bad guys and opt for flexible exchange rates as offering a better alternative, with less disruptive adjustment and with less danger of destabilizing speculation, than the adjustable peg.

Another line of thought is suggested to me by Mr. Solomon's remarks on balance-of-payments objectives. If we insist on stating the problem in terms of how large a current surplus a country wants to run—with Germany, say, wanting a yearly surplus of $3 billion or $4 billion—we can only be appalled by the complex combination of policy measures and the extensive international cooperation that would be required. But the need for such balance-of-payments objectives simply disappears with flexible rates. The flexible-rate system enables us to attend to the more important objectives, such as full employment, undistracted by the balance of payments, which, no longer an object of policy, becomes merely a residual adjusted by movements of the exchange rate.

My next comment is in reply to Robert Triffin's objections to fluctuating rates. He said that a temporary deficit will mean unwanted changes in exchange rates. I would suggest that this conclusion overlooks the role of speculators in such a situation. A temporary deficit, if it were foreseeable—and many such deficits would be foreseeable—would be taken care of by a stabilizing type of speculation, with little or no movement in the exchange rate. Triffin's other objection was that if a country were to engage in overspending, this would induce rate fluctuations that were also inappropriate. I would raise the question, why shouldn't there be rate fluctuations if a country indulges in overspending? Such a depreciation of a currency in the face of overspending would be a red light indicating that the country was engaging in inflationary activity.

Many people seem to fear that flexible rates would result in continuous bobbing up and down of rates all over the place. I think these people overlook the probable emergence of optimal currency areas. Quite naturally, countries would band together; Western European countries might agree to stabilize their rates among themselves, other countries would stabilize on the dollar, and currency areas would emerge that were more or less optimal.

A final word about managed flexible rates, which I would suggest have real dangers. J. E. Meade some time back made a suggestion in this connection which seems to me useful—namely, that the IMF could play a helpful role in a flexible-rate regime as a counter-speculator. If a country engaged in deliberate competitive depreciation, then the IMF, using its stabilization funds, could step in and counteract such activity.

CONRAD C. JAMISON: In recent years, we have drifted from crisis to crisis in the international monetary sphere, with the threat always present of a major breakdown in the entire mechanism. Clearly, something has to be done. The present system in practice, if not entirely in theory, is one of undue rigidity. Pressures build higher and higher until eventually we have an earthquake. We need a system that will permit pressures to be released gradually and intermittently, so that we can reach equilibrium with only minor tremors instead of a major upheaval.

When a nation consistently runs deficits in its international payments, it is of course possible for it to correct the situation by internal adjustments—that is, by means of restrictive and deflationary policies affecting its economy. This correction could be induced by an international system whereby these measures are imposed from the outside, as under the old gold standard, except that, as a practical matter, few if any nations would tolerate surrender of sovereignty of this nature. The correction could be voluntary on the part of the nation running the deficit, except that, again, as a practical matter, few nations would surrender their domestic goals for this reason, nor would they voluntarily exercise the degree of self-discipline that is necessary.

Consequently, the most feasible answer would appear to be greater flexibility in exchange rates, though the answer would *not* appear to be freely floating exchange rates. Ideally, the latter policy may have great appeal—indeed, it has great appeal to me—but I think that once more, for practical reasons, we have to settle for something considerably less than freely floating rates. Moreover, I think the international mechanism desperately needs stability and predictability in exchange rates as well as a greater degree of flexibility. These aims are not completely incompatible; I am confident that a reasonable compromise can be worked out. The compromise we need would appear to be a modification of the present system which would permit both a wider band of fluctuation and adjustable pegs, adjustments which would be moderate in size. Then we could have the best of two worlds—both flexibility and reasonable stability.

SIDNEY S. ALEXANDER: I had hoped to come here to learn something, and I had intended not to speak, because I have found that one doesn't learn much with one's mouth open. But I think that there are some problems both with the existing system and with the leading contender, flexible exchange rates, that have not been fully explored.

Taking the present system first, the problem with the jumping peg is that it balks at the hurdle. A jumper that doesn't jump is not very useful. It's not that the jumping peg is a bad system; like Christianity, it has hardly been tried—the adjustments simply aren't being made.

With respect to flexible rates, I would like to say what the famous Archie the Cockroach said about ghosts: "I don't believe in them; you wouldn't either if you knew as many as I do." The problem with a flexible rate is that is sounds good; as certain speakers have said, exchange rates are prices and prices should be flexible, but what kind of price does a flexible rate resemble? Does it resemble a price for a single good in the standard micro-economic market, or is it more like the price level equilibrating for inflation? For a single good, we have reason to believe that a price will equilibrate a market very well, but it is far from clear that an exchange rate will be as successful in equilibrating the market for foreign currencies. Indeed, it may even be that, when capital movements are brought into the picture, a flexible rate may actually be destabilizing, or there may be a penumbra (to use Taussig's term) within which it may be destabilizing. Professor Aliber's interpretation of the French experience in the 1920's is essentially along that line. Whether he is right or not, I don't know, but I certainly believe that things could happen that way.

Thus exchange-rate fluctuation may be a fairly weak instrument of equilibration if, indeed, it is an instrument of equilibration at all. It may even be a destabilizing factor, and that leads me to the feeling that some problems are really problems. Given the constraints that we have all admitted—that we don't want to deflate when we have a deficit, that we don't want monetary policy tied to the balance of payments, and so on—it may be just as difficult to get things to work under flexible exchanges as it is now. I think that the problem of international adjustment goes much deeper than being merely a matter of exchange-rate policy.

JOHN EXTER: My thinking on international adjustment is dominated by what I regard as the overwhelming importance of monetary policy. I see in expanding paper money the dangerously explosive properties of dynamite. It can destroy the kind of world in which we want to live. I became monetarily unhappy as far back as 1958. As long ago as early 1962, Paul Samuelson quipped, "Well, John, you could be right, but you are lonely." Here today, only Michael Heilperin has expressed views like mine, so I feel less lonely, but I suspect that we are a minority of two.

My economic model is so different from those of speakers other than Michael that I need a little time to describe it. Please visualize the monetary system of the entire world as a pyramid—an upside-down pyramid whose pinnacle becomes the base. The base is gold owned by central banks. Banks create credit—note and deposit liabilities which people use as money—whenever they add to their assets. In this way central banks created credit when they acquired the gold. They have also created credit by acquiring other assets. But all assets other than gold are paper—paper IOU's. Think of the pyramid as including not only all central banks and all currencies of the world but also all debtors and creditors—you and me, Mr. Jamison's Security Pacific National Bank, my bank, the IMF, General Motors, everyone.

The pyramid has two basic constraints. First, currencies in it are interlocked at fixed exchange rates, are freely convertible into each other at those rates, and are directly or indirectly convertible into gold at the base at $35 an ounce. Second, each debtor in it is required to pay his debts.

There are three reasons for thinking of the system as an upside-down pyramid. The first is most important. When a central bank like our Federal Reserve becomes expansionist—that is, creates notes and deposits against paper assets—it lends the newly created deposits, for example, to our government by buying U. S. government securities, thus increasing debt. In our fractional reserve system, the created deposits become excess reserves of member banks, which in turn can create deposits on their books and lend them to business, consumers, governments, and customers overseas, again increasing debt. Credit creation spreads in the world, and debt grows faster than production. In the last ten years, private debt in the United States grew 38 percent more rapidly than gross national product. The additional debt created by lending newly created deposits cannot be serviced and repaid from ordinary economic growth—growth resulting from rising productivity. To enable the servicing and repayment, the Federal Reserve must create more money in the second year than in the first, more in the third than in the second, and so on, thus building the credit pyramid. In 1960, when the pyramid was smaller, the Federal Reserve acquired about half a billion dollars of paper assets; in 1968, when it was large, about $5 billion. Hence the pyramid's explosiveness.

The second reason for its shape is that, as the pyramid grows, interest rates rise. In the early 1960's, the discount rate was 3 percent and the prime rate 4½ percent. Today these rates are 5½ percent and 7 percent. The burden of debt rises, but the cost of servicing it rises too, and contributes to the pyramid shape.

Third, a time comes in the growth of the pyramid when resources are fully employed, and costs and prices rise. It may cost General Motors half again as much to build a plant today as ten years ago; so it must find half again as much money. Thus inflation also contributes to the pyramid shape.

All is well as long as the pyramid continues to grow, but like a tree, it cannot grow to the sky. A time comes when creditors in it begin to think that important debtors cannot pay. The debtors can be arrayed according to their liquidity, the most liquid being down near the gold base and the least liquid at the very top—particularly those who have borrowed short while lending and investing long.

When creditors lose confidence in the illiquid debtors at the top, they refuse to lend them more or leave them altogether and run down the pyramid to more liquid debtors and to gold. If debtors cannot pay, there will be debt liquidation. Creditors ran from the Bank of England in November 1967 and converted sterling into other currencies and gold. When the Bank of England could not pay, the pound was devalued, thus liquidating 14.3 percent of sterling liabilities in the pyramid. Next the market took $35 gold from the Federal Reserve and, indeed, from even the liquid central banks—almost $3 billion between November 1967 and March 1968—thereby shrinking the gold base of the pyramid.

In March 1968, all central banks except the South African decided not to pay; they closed their gold windows to private people and began the two-tier system, another liquidation of debt in the pyramid. More crises followed, and many more are yet to come.

For today's credit pyramid has become, by all odds, the largest in history, and it is still growing. In my view, it is now too large to be consistent with its two basic constraints. The constraint of fixed exchange rates cannot be maintained much longer, for illiquid central banks are less and less able and willing to defend their rates with gold—$35 gold. When they do not defend them with gold, they must borrow from other central banks, particularly the more liquid. But if the lenders cannot expect payment in gold, they will ultimately limit their lending, in which case exchange rates must go. It is idle to think that crawling pegs, wider bands, or what have you, will solve this dilemma. In fact, they will more likely accentuate it. In the real world, the immediate prospect is more frequent changes in fixed exchange rates or perhaps even floating rates.

The far more serious problem of the credit pyramid is the second constraint, especially since many illiquid debtors other than central banks around the world will one day be unable to pay their debts. Then the pyramid may cease to grow or even enter a period of liquidation. Today's rapidly rising interest rates, despite rapid credit expansion, signal a massive worldwide liquidity squeeze.

Chairman THORP: John raises an interesting question: How many angels can sit on the top of a pyramid?

EXTER: They're not angels up there; the angels are at the bottom.

ROBERT OLIVER: I would like to divide my remarks into two parts—first, a few words about the Bretton Woods system and, second, a few words about how this system relates to the adjustment process itself.

The first point I wish to make about the system is that the reserves which materialized in the Bretton Woods Agreement were much smaller than the amount proposed by the British in the Keynes Plan. Moreover, the reserves proposed in both the Keynes and the White Plans were not national currency reserves per se. Thus, there is a sense in which we can say that international reserves have been inadequate since

1944. This fact was obscured as the dollar came to be used as a reserve asset, but the use of the dollar as a reserve asset has, of course, imposed severe restrictions on the freedom of action of the United States.

My second point about the Bretton Woods system is that it should be viewed in terms of all of its original objectives. Professor Jacob Viner in 1944 wrote that the objectives were to make trade barriers as moderate and nondiscriminatory as possible, to secure reasonably stable exchange rates and freely convertible currencies, to encourage the movement of long-term capital from capital-rich to capital-poor areas, to provide for international collaboration aimed at high-level employment, and, in general, to increase the scope of competitive free enterprise. By all these standards, it seems to me that the system, at least from 1955 to 1965, would have to be judged a substantial success. The 8 percent yearly increase in trade and the even larger increase in the flow of long-term capital are facts which we ought to take into account in evaluating both the system and the adjustment process itself.

My third point about the system is that the spectacular aberrations of recent years, which have received such publicity and have caused such difficulty, have been due primarily to an unwillingness to devalue on the part of countries with overvalued currencies, or to devalue in time; and this is important. In our deliberations, perhaps we should ask ourselves why devaluation has proved to be so difficult. In my view, the biggest deficiency of the Bretton Woods system has been the lack of an agreed mechanism for decreasing the value of the dollar relative to other currencies. Since this point has been referred to by other participants but has not been discussed explicitly, I would hope that we can later talk about the problem of changing the exchange rate of the dollar.

The overvalued dollar problem has been exacerbated by the use of both dollars and gold as reserves at a fixed price. A way out of this difficulty would be either to raise the price of gold, as suggested by Sir Roy Harrod, thus in effect driving gold back into Fort Knox and making the dollar standard work, or else to sever completely the tie between the dollar and gold. I take it that most of those who advocate raising the price of gold regard the action as a second-best solution, but I wonder what our position would be on this proposal if, instead of South Africa, it were Canada or the United Kingdom or the United States which happened to own all the supplies of newly mined gold.

A few words, if I may, on the adjustment process per se. We all agree that the process will be difficult, regardless of the system in effect, as long as reserves are so low that many nations will seek payments surpluses to increase their reserves and as long as reserves are increasing at an inadequate rate. Moreover, for nations which—to use Professor Triffin's language—have been overspending for a fair amount of time, adjustment to a lower level of expenditure is not going to be painless and is going to impose a serious political problem during the adjustment process. No system is going to remove all the pain or all the political friction, and under any system we are simply going to have to put up with ad hoc measures which attempt to cope with political realities.

Finally, it seems to me that in talking about the adjustment mechanism we need to say something about over-all international objectives. I would again suggest that the continued growth of trade and flow of capital are very important objectives which should not be interfered with by whatever adjustment mechanism is used. I would add that price-level stability and full employment are also important goals for an international system. These conclusions lead me to the observation that sometimes the onus of adjustment should be on the surplus nation and sometimes it should be on the deficit nation; but I do not see how, a priori, we can tell which of the two needs to do the adjusting until we have a clear idea of what the international system should be trying to accomplish.

ALICE BOURNEUF: I've been getting more and more worried this afternoon, because I am definitely not on the side of the angels, and I don't know where I'm going to end up.

I can't help thinking that, as a practical matter for the major countries, there is no substitute for once-and-for-all, or jumping, exchange-rate adjustments—that is, for the adjustable peg. By this, I mean adjustments made after the best possible estimates of the change needed, adjustments announced with indications that the new rate will be given all possible support. The arguments for new exchange-rate systems—fluctuating rates, wider bands, crawling pegs, and so forth—seem to be either unrealistic for the foreseeable future or overly optimistic; and they all seem to be based on the assumption that reasonable jumps in exchange rates cannot be brought about.

In my opinion, the adoption of freely fluctuating exchange rates, whatever may be their theoretical advantages, is simply not a practical possibility for the major leading currencies. Treasury officials, central bankers, and members of legislative bodies don't seem to be prepared for such a move, and, if one can judge by the wrangling that went on during the congressional hearings on Bretton Woods, American congressmen will never be won over to a system of freely fluctuating exchange rates.

I am not much more optimistic about wider bands. The wider band has the advantage that it at least does not destroy faith in the stability of the basic par, but I am not sure how successful it would be in the present situation, with several major countries in persistent payments difficulties and with control of capital movements ineffective. Given the present situation, it would seem likely that the initial effect would simply be that the currencies of the major countries would go to the limit of the band, or just short of it. A 10 percent change might be big enough to have important corrective effects, but it seems to me that large destabilizing capital movements would be fed under this system, and there would be no implication, as under the adjustable-peg system, that the change in rate was decided upon and deemed to be reasonable.

Clearly, the wider band would not provide a continuing mechanism of adjustment in cases of persistent balance-of-payments difficulty. Persistent pressures in the same direction would require some additional mechanism. If the additional mechanism were a crawling peg, it might be that even greater destabilizing effects would result. Moreover, the whole question of the extent to which reserves and drawing rights would be used to support a rate at any given time would seem to be up in the air.

As Mr. Southard suggested, governments do like to leave exchange rates alone. Wider margins, combined with a crawling peg, would seem to have some of the disadvantages of the fixed-rate system, at least between crawls, and to just miss the theoretical advantages of the freely fluctuating rate. I can't help wishing that the energy now being devoted to new exchange-rate schemes were being devoted to trying to solve the problem of how to get government officials to make once-and-for-all necessary exchange-rate adjustments.

In the area of fiscal policy, we have accepted ad hoc shifts in tax policies to achieve full employment, but we have not yet agreed to, or obtained, automatic tax-rate flexibility. The analogy in the exchange-rate field would seem to be to get government officials to accept occasional exchange-rate adjustments before trying to get complete exchange-rate flexibility. I don't think that automatic rules for the timing of exchange-rate changes, based on changes in reserves or similar rules of thumb, can solve the problem. The real job is to sell the national policy-makers on the advantages of exchange-rate changes, just as they have finally been sold on the advantages of a rational fiscal policy.

SEYMOUR E. HARRIS: The first point I want to make is that the $1.6 billion surplus in the U. S. balance of payments in 1968 (on a reserve-transactions basis) does not mean that we are out of the woods. In particular, the price-cost situation continues to deteriorate. From 1960 to 1964, the consumer price level rose only 3 percent; from 1964 to 1968, it rose 13 percent. Under the new administration, the policy apparently is to keep inflation down, but not at the sacrifice of high levels of employment. Incidentally, I might say that, looking at the Nixon program, we should welcome the President into the New Economics Club. Since I coined the term "new economics" right after the war, I think I can speak with some authority on that subject. There are questions about the Nixon program—in particular, whether we can keep inflation down without bringing about some reduction in output. But it seems clear to me that the economic objectives of the new administration, and the means of achieving those objectives, are pretty much the same as under President Johnson.

I think there is a good possibility that the present administration will have less inflation that the last one, though it will probably mean more unemployment. One possibility for a reduction in inflationary pressure is in the field of welfare expenditures, which increased from $50 billion in 1960 to $112 billion in 1968. Seven-eighths of this increase is attributable to the federal government. I would guess that under the Nixon administration welfare expenditures will not continue to grow at this rate.

One important general point I want to make is that, in the early years of the Kennedy administration, a new theory developed in Washington that the greater the U.S. economic growth rate, the better the U.S. balance of payments would be. That is contrary to the old classical theory, as we all know. I was fairly critical of this new theory, of which Jim Tobin was one of the authors. But I confess there is something to it. The difference between the Tobin theory and the classical theory is that Tobin was taking account of capital movements. What he was really saying is that even though growth may have an unfavorable effect on the trade balance because of the increase in imports, there is likely to be a net gain in the over-all balance of payments, since the favorable economic climate will attract a large inflow of capital from abroad. And that is what has happened to a considerable extent recently.

Turning to another subject, I do believe there is a good deal in what Sir Roy Harrod says about the price of gold. We have to have more liquidity. If we can get it in some other way, good, but if we can't, then we ought to consider seriously the Harrod proposal. There is only one objection I would have to Sir Roy's proposal, and that is that it doesn't deal with the problem of the competitive position of the United States. It deals with the general problem, but it doesn't deal with the overvaluation of the dollar, and we should devote some of our attention to that particular problem.

JOHN PARKE YOUNG: There are several monetary facts of life that we cannot get away from. First, so long as we have a variety of independent currency systems, there are bound to be problems of value relationships among the different currencies. Second, the nature of the adjustment problem and the determination of appropriate adjustment mechanisms depend to a large extent upon goals and priorities. They also depend upon the nature of the world monetary system. This system has changed greatly in recent decades with the development of the gold (dollar) exchange standard, the decline in the role of gold, central bank credit extensions, currency swaps, cooperation, and so on. It is in the process of further major change. Third, the optimum currency area is, I believe, the entire world. But even if we did have a single currency, we would still have an adjustment problem—

namely, that of payments among regions. It would be of a different kind and related to such things as factor mobility among regions, but the adjustment problem would still be with us. A fourth and controlling fact is that the world is not politically ready for the kind of monetary system it really needs. World trade and interdependence have outgrown the present monetary system before we were able to bring into being a system adapted to present-day needs. We must face the unpleasant fact that, for the present, we cannot work out the kind of monetary system we would like to see; we must accept political realities.

Where do we go from here? In particular, what do we do about exchange rates, which are a major factor in adjustment? Under the fixed-rate system, we try to adjust payments to a particular exchange rate rather than to adjust the rate to payments. The latter is basically what is needed. The essence of the problem is how best to keep the rate in reasonable harmony with the underlying payments situation in an inflation-prone world with continuing structural changes and large, often unpredictable, capital flows. One difficulty with the present so-called jumping rate, as Professor Alexander pointed out, is that the rate does not always jump when it should. Moreover, the prospect of a jump, and the jump when it does occur, can be quite disturbing.

I believe that we must find a way of introducing into the system more exchange-rate flexibility. Rates have been entirely too rigid. But when we come to the question of how to achieve more flexibility, we find difficulties with all the alternatives. Some form of the crawling peg is probably the best compromise for currencies other than the dollar, which should continue as the anchor.

We want full employment, growth, and price stability, and we don't want an exchange-rate policy that interferes with these goals or that hampers trade and investment. We want the best of all worlds and are confronted with the need to reconcile the irreconcilable. Whether or not we agree on the priority of goals doesn't make much difference, because governments simply are not going to incur substantial unemployment for balance-of-payments reasons.

In dealing with the problem of international adjustment, we need to strengthen and expand the role of the International Monetary Fund. The Fund must be given more authority, if necessary by amending the Articles of Agreement, not only to permit greater exchange-rate flexibility but to develop stronger consultation procedures. We recall the original arguments over an automatic versus a discretionary Fund. A combination of the two approaches, involving considerable automatic member rights coupled with strong Fund authority, is possible and desirable. The Fund is developing along this line.

Despite political difficulties, the Group of Ten must eventually be brought largely under the IMF, which was intended to be the final authority in the international monetary field. An orchestra with two conductors does not give the best music. A solution may be along the lines of several regional groups with regional responsibilities.

There are other aspects of the Fund which call for change. For example, I think there's a good deal to be said in favor of pooling reserves in an IMF reserve-settlement account in order to discourage switching from one form of reserve to another. The various proposals of this kind have merit.

We should also consider, as a long-run policy, what we are going to do about further development of the Special Drawing Rights—in particular, whether we should look forward to and hasten the development of SDR's as the principal, and eventually the only, international reserve asset, thereby getting rid of national currencies and ultimately even gold as reserves. Gold continues its gradual trend toward the monetary grave, despite its present role on the world stage and appearance of strength. We can help direct this trend, as was done in setting up the two-tier arrangement.

Finally, what do we do about border taxes, import quotas, export subsidies, and investment controls as means of adjustment? I think we must find better ways of dealing with adjustment difficulties. Such devices are harmful to trade, and they distort the allocation of resources. We should try to develop a system under which we don't have to resort to these dubious expedients. In pursuing this task, we need to recognize, as I said before, that no completely satisfactory system is politically feasible. We must work out the most satisfactory compromise we can in a far from satisfactory world.

CHAPTER IV

DIALOGUE ON THE OPTIONS: CHOICES IN EXCHANGE-RATE POLICY

From the first day's dialogue on general issues, it was abundantly clear that the topic which was the target of greatest attention and interest was the broad area of exchange-rate policy. On this matter, there was nothing approaching a consensus. Various proposals were advanced, and each was supported by some and rejected by others. Accordingly, it was agreed that the second day of the conference should be devoted exclusively to the role of exchange-rate policy in international adjustment. The present chapter is a record of the day's deliberations.

R. H.

Chairman THORP: We have agreed to devote our attention today to the problem of how to improve the adjustment process through exchange-rate policy. This opens up a great number of different questions, and I would like to suggest a pattern to be followed in our discussion.

First, there are certain matters I hope we won't discuss. I think we would all agree that, in the final analysis, any solution which we as economists think may be desirable still has to pass the test of being politically acceptable. Important as that may be, I suggest that we not spend our time, or take our positions, on the basis of whether or not a given proposal is politically possible at the present time. This is not the field of our expertise and, in any case, it is useful to consider what is first-best in economic terms rather than to start with second-best.

There is another matter on which I think we agree—namely, that frequently a particular line of action which looks good in one place at one time may not provide a general solution. Something which may seem to be a good adjustment technique when a country is in suplus may not apply to deficit countries, and vice versa. Moreover, we must regard the United States as a special case. It is quite possible that any system we set up may not provide the same opportunities to the United States that it would to other countries. This point was made by several members yesterday and, while it clearly needs to be kept in mind, requires no further elaboration.

There are certain other questions on which we did not agree yesterday which I would suggest we also set aside, as they could easily divert our attention from our central theme. Among these is the question of whether the U. S. dollar is or is not overvalued and the question of whether the international monetary system is or is not on the verge of collapse. We could spend many hours discussing these matters, but our problem is *adjustment.* I would suggest that we concentrate on central questions of exchange-rate policy, because we are all agreed—I don't think anyone has taken a contrary position—that there must be exchange-rate changes in whatever system there is, including of course the Bretton Woods system, which explicitly provides for changes in parities.

The question is how often, how much, and how general. Here we have a broad spectrum of positions. Some members of the conference have presented the argument that the present system, if one can call it a system, can be improved, but that fundamentally we ought to continue thinking of ourselves as living in a world of fixed exchange rates—of rates which may be adjusted from time to time but which remain pegged until such adjustments are made. This would be a position of minimal change. It would be a position of trying to work within the present structure, but recognizing the need for improvements of one sort or another. A considerable number of those around this table have indicated that a minor repair job isn't good enough, and therefore we have such suggestions as a wider band, a crawling peg, and other ways of permitting flexibility within limits, the limits being necessary to avoid sudden wide changes. This would be an intermediate position. Finally, there were members yesterday who suggested that we really ought to go the whole hog. Why this intermediate business? Why not really move to exchange-rate flexibility? This extreme position would let the exchange rate be a price free to move like any other price, but some who think along these lines would prefer to have the rate managed somewhat.

I would hope that today we could start our discussion with the notion of working within the fixed-rate system, and see what changes are possible while remaining within that system. I don't think we should spend too much time on this alternative, because it is probably more important for us to examine the proposed innovations and see how they might work. So after a brief consideration of the position of minimal change, I hope we can move on and consider the problems and possibilities arising from the proposals for the wider band, the crawling peg, Bob Triffin's new set of prongs, and other suggestions for limited flexibility. Finally, we can examine what one might call the natural position of the economist—that the exchange rate should be allowed complete, or almost complete, freedom of movement in order to perform the same function as any other price in equating supply and demand.

To start, I have asked Eddie Bernstein to open the discussion by indicating from his rich experience, so closely related to the IMF and exchange-rate matters, his views on how well the present system has been working.

BERNSTEIN: Before we decide that we need radical surgery, it might be well to examine the health of the patient to see whether tender love and care wouldn't accomplish all that is really needed.

In the discussion yesterday, Professor Allen cited a statement I made at the Bologna conference to the effect that the adjustment process is of course the big problem, that we only talk about liquidity because it is related to the adjustment problem, and that the adjustment process has worked reasonably well except in the case of those two dubiously clad "emperors," the United States and the United Kingdom. I think it is important to bear in mind that if our problem is the United States and the United Kingdom, or the United States alone, it may be susceptible to a different type of solution than changing the whole system.

But let's examine what has really happened under the Fund regime. As I said yesterday, the Bretton Woods system contemplates that countries will have a balanced position over time, that they will have surpluses and deficits that alternate, and that they will be given time to adjust their deficits, so that they will not have to take harsh deflationary measures or to impose restrictions on trade and payments that would undermine international prosperity. Implicit in this philosophy is the theory that surpluses and deficits are in large measure the by-product of cyclical fluctuations, and that if a deficit country will take steps, not to deflate the economy, but just to stop the inflation, it will experience a sharp improvement in the trade balance and in the balance of payments as a whole.

Is there any truth to this? Indeed there is. We have a considerable number of cases in which countries have experienced very sharp changes in the trade balance within very short periods following their own changes in policy. For example, a few years ago Italy had a bad balance of payments. According to the London *Economist*, there was no solution except to devalue the lira. And what happened? A restrictive credit policy, within twelve or thirteen months, transformed a trade deficit running at an annual rate of well over $1 billion into a trade surplus of around $2 billion. Today we talk about Italy as the second big surplus country after Germany.

Take the case of Japan. Japan is a country which is growing so fast that any overshooting of the investment market at home is bound to bring a balance-of-payments deficit. Not long ago, the Japanese had a serious payments problem, and people asked me if I thought the yen could be held at its present parity. The Japanese, being a stubborn people, would have held the yen regardless of whether I thought it could or couldn't be held, but the fact of the matter is that last year the Japanese had an over-all payments surplus of close to $1 billion, the largest they have ever had.

And take the case of Germany itself. In 1965 the German trade surplus was close to zero, the current account was in deficit, and there was an over-all deficit of well over $1 billion. This all changed, of course, as soon as the boom ended. Today, four years later, we are talking about a German surplus which is destructive of the capacity of other countries to adjust their balances of payments. I think there is considerable merit in this contention, but the point I want to make now is that a quick reversal is possible. One reason it is possible is that the great trading countries have become excellent substitutes for each other in supplying many types of manufactured goods.

Thus, history is not really against the Fund concept that most balance-of-payments adjustment can be accomplished reasonably well through changing the trade balance by proper policies—without deflation. I would not agree with Professor Aliber, who said yesterday that countries really don't care about the international aspects of their policies. That is not true, except perhaps in the United States and, to a limited extent, in the United Kingdom, where some economists hold strongly to the dogma that the balance of payments must not dictate domestic policy.

Let me now go on to another aspect of the problem of adjustment. Of course, a country that has had a long continued inflation is bound to find that inflation imbedded in its prices and costs. This situation may even generate a continuous active inflation, where people get so accustomed to having 10 percent wage increases to offset the inflation of the past, the inflation of the present, and often the inflation they expect in the future, that stability is unattainable. But if a country has undermined the relationship of prices and costs, the Bretton Woods philosophy recognizes that there is no proper alternative to a change in parity.

It is astonishing how much difference of opinion there was at Bretton Woods among reasonably intelligent people on how much use would be made of changes in parity. Keynes was so sure that changes would take place frequently that he even wanted to make them automatic. After a country had reached a certain deficit position, it would have to devalue its currency. Mr. Rasminsky, now Governor of the Bank of Canada, was of the opinion that, in fact, the real problem was not going to be competitive devaluation but rather an unwillingness of countries to change their parities. On the whole, I think historical experience has shown that Rasminsky was nearer right than Keynes.

At the same time, as I indicated yesterday, even the developed countries have made considerable use of exchange-rate changes as a method of adjustment under the Bretton Woods system. I would add that, excluding the United Kingdom, whose recent delay in adjusting the sterling parity was destructive, the resistance to frequent changes in parity has not been entirely bad. In fact, this resistance is an important element in the stability of the international monetary system. I think there is something useful in having countries reluctant to change their rates and willing to say, "Let's try stopping the inflation first."

My next point concerns structural change. We professors—

and I include myself as an ex-professor—like to focus on difficult cases. And in truth the Bretton Woods system has no easy solution to problems of structural change. This doesn't mean that there is no solution. Ordinarily, structural changes are slow changes, and one way in which adjustment can take place is to have a rise in wage rates slightly greater than the increase in productivity in countries that are gaining in relative international position—and therefore tend to be in surplus—while having wage increases slightly less than the increase in productivity in other countries.

That, of course, is not an easy prescription to carry out. But, in my opinion, it is not difficult to show that in Germany wage rates are too low in relation to productivity. Obviously, in any country with a persistent payments surplus, prices and costs are too low relative to those abroad. What is significant is that, within Germany, wages are too low relative to productivity in the sense that labor is getting too small a share of the national product. The share of consumption in the GNP of Germany is the lowest of any large industrial country except Japan, which has about the same share; and my guess is that wages are too low relative to productivity in Japan as well as in Germany.

My concluding point is that, in those cases where the Bretton Woods system has not worked well, ways have been found of coping with the situation. Of course, the Fund Articles of Agreement contemplated exchange controls when necessary, and such controls have proved to be necessary from time to time. While there is not time here to go into the question of how much harm is done by exchange control on capital transactions, I don't mind giving you my own view that it does very little harm—that what the controls do is to compel investors to seek funds elsewhere at a slightly higher interest rate. I don't think our investment abroad, in real terms, has been much affected by the controls; all the controls have done is to shift the financing and, in some degree, to raise the cost.

The Fund was almost the first institution to recognize that import surcharges are a convenient way to deal with payments problems, particularly for the less developed countries. The Fund has also been lenient with the less developed countries in permitting the use of multiple exchange rates. In fact, multiple rates in some cases are equivalent to surcharges on imports, while in other cases they are equivalent to bounties on exports. In my opinion, the Fund would probably take the view that import surcharges, when combined with tax refunds for exports, are de facto devaluations, or rather partial devaluations which apply only to the trade account—and often to only part of that. Thus, one can justify these measures to the extent—and only to the extent—that one can justify multiple exchange rates.

With respect to fluctuating exchange rates, the Fund has been exceedingly tolerant for an institution built on the principle of fixed parities. I can recall Fund papers expounding fluctuating rates (a) for less developed countries that simply can't keep up with the change in raw-material prices; (b) for big industrial countries that need a change in parity but aren't sure what the new parity should be, and therefore want a transitional testing period; and (c) for countries, like Canada, which feel that they are unable, by other means, to cope with the capital-inflow problems that beset them. In my opinion, it would not be difficult to persuade the Fund to accept more exchange-rate flexibility, as it has always shown great tolerance in that direction. But I would remind you that no system of greater flexibility is going to work unless we stop inflation. And if we stop the inflation, do we need so much more flexibility than we now have?

HANSEN: What do you mean by inflation—a rise in prices of 3 percent a year?

BERNSTEIN: Well, what price level are you talking about? I agree that some rise in consumer prices is perfectly natural, as the consumer price level includes services and taxes.

HANSEN: What index are you using?

BERNSTEIN: I'm using wholesale prices of domestically produced industrial goods.

HANSEN: A 3 percent rise in your index—is that inflation or not?

BERNSTEIN: You put in your own figure, Alvin; I have no objection. It has to meet your test; if not, it won't work. That is my point: In a world with an inflationary bias, a fixed-rate system won't work; a flexible-rate system won't work well, but it might work a little better than a fixed-rate system.

HABERLER: A number of interesting questions have been raised. Broadly speaking, I agree with Eddie Bernstein that the Bretton Woods system has worked. The growth of world trade has been tremendous, even during the past two years when so many new controls have been imposed, and by that standard one might be inclined to be satisfied and to say that nothing need be changed.

But I am not quite sure that this is the right way of looking at the matter. The good very often is the enemy of the better, and there is, of course, the danger that the good record may not last very long. It is true that in some cases the mechanism of fixed exchanges has worked well—I would even say a little too well for the comfort of others. Both in Italy and in Germany, a serious payments deficit was corrected without a change in the exchange rate. The Italian experience in the early 1960's is of special interest, in that a leftist government allowed the central bank to step on the brake. In Germany, the system of fixed exchanges has worked too well in view of the enormous surpluses of the last two years.

Most people would agree, I believe, that there have been at least two cases recently where a change in the exchange rate should have been made; the French franc should have been depreciated and the German mark should have gone up. These changes were resisted; instead, the two countries used the messy substitute of border taxes and tax refunds for exporters, and there are very few people who believe that these makeshifts will work.*

Is it possible, in the framework of the IMF as we have it under the adjustable peg, to compel necessary changes in exchange rates? I must say I doubt it. I am afraid this matter takes us into the political sphere, but we cannot avoid that altogether. For it is one of the defects of the present system that any change in an exchange rate has become a major political operation. What we ought to have is a system whereby this method of adjustment is taken out of politics. That is exactly the purpose of the wider band and the crawling peg: to make possible needed changes in exchange rates and to keep them out of politics.

I should add that there is another serious difficulty with the present system of the adjustable peg. Even if we could overcome the political resistance to a change in parity, we

*On this matter, Professor Haberler was clearly vindicated by the course of events. Later in 1969, both of the "resisted" changes in exchange rates took place.—R.H.

would have the problem in every single case that we don't know by how much a country should appreciate or depreciate. Thus the change in rate always comes too late and, at least in the case of depreciation, is usually too great, because, as we all know, it is better to err on the side of depreciating too much rather than too little. In actual fact, the Bretton Woods system has become a fixed-rate system, and I wish that those like Professor Bloomfield and Professor Bourneuf, who uphold the present system, would deal with these arguments, which I am sure they have thought about.

Now a word on inflation. Eddie Bernstein and Sidney Alexander say, quite rightly, that no system will work well with inflation, but I agree with Alvin Hansen that we have to be a little more precise. Take the United States. The United States has not had much inflation. Except for the last two or three years, the U. S. consumer-price index has risen less than that of any other country in the world except Venezuela and one or two of the Central American countries. Despite this fact, we have had all these troubles.

BERNSTEIN: But you're measuring inflation by the price rise; inflation has to be measured by the excess demand which is in itself manifested in two separate ways, by a decline in the export surplus . . .

HABERLER: Do you think we can have inflation without any price rise? Excess demand? What does excess demand mean? Here it means that you buy too much and sell too little, so it is just a definition of the deficit in the balance of payments. From a policy standpoint, I still think that the price level is the important thing, and not such a nebulous and tautological concept as excess demand.

Chairman THORP: On this particular issue, I'm going to ask Judge Alexander to give us his comment.

ALEXANDER: One word, terminological. Mark Twain said you could always have a good argument on either two names for the same thing or two things for the same name. The concept I would prefer to use is aggregate demand. And whether we have inflation in the sense of a price rise depends upon whether we have a constraint in the foreign market. Clearly, given any excessive increase in aggregate demand, if we have the reserves to get from abroad that which meets the demand, we need not have a price rise. Do we call that inflation or not? I don't care. The problem, however, is an aggregate demand for more resources than are domestically produced, so that if you talk about inflation, you can become confused between the effect of inflation and the cause of inflation. Separate the two.

HARROD: Unless we get a clear distinction, the whole of this discussion is worthless. There are many definitions of inflation. One of the better is the rise of factor prices. We've had a good deal of inflation of that kind. Totally different is the excess demand of Keynes, of which we've had very little in the United Kingdom since 1955; it was largely before that. And actually, if you take the trend, the rise of factor prices has been steeper in the United Kingdom in the years in which the Keynesian excess demand has been less. Unless we keep these two concepts absolutely separate in our heads, we will get nowhere.

BERNSTEIN: I must ask permission to clarify my position so that people will understand what I am saying. By inflation, I mean aggregate demand which increases more than the community can supply in increased output without getting the price rise I have been talking about—the rise in wholesale prices of industrial goods. The excess demand will then spill over into import goods if a country can pay for them, and I can conceive of a situation where the excess demand grows so little and the import demand is so elastic that the country's price level is stable even though demand remains excessive. What happens is that it all goes into the import surplus. So I am, in fact, using the excess-demand test, and I am saying that excess demand can manifest itself in two separate ways—in the wholesale-price level and in the import surplus.

Chairman THORP: I think we can move on now, so that we can hear from others around the table. Dick Cooper is next.

RICHARD N. COOPER: I would like to take issue with Eddie Bernstein on his interpretation of what has happened over the last two decades. I agree with him that the world economy has done spectacularly well: I think there is no question about that by any historical standard. But the international economy has not been on the Bretton Woods system throughout the whole postwar period; in fact, it did not go on to that system, really, until around 1960.

During the 1950's, we did have a process of adjustment in spite of the commitment to fixed exchange rates. The process involved differential trade and capital-movement liberalization, especially by the European countries. As their payments positions improved, countries liberalized trade, removed quotas, and relaxed other restraints on international transactions. And they liberalized at a differential rate, thus keeping the world economy in better balance than would have been possible if we had started out in the immediate postwar period with the ideal Bretton Woods system—that is, a system free of direct restrictions on trade and other current transactions. The liberalization process, as I have said, was differential, France moving ahead rather faster when its payments position improved rapidly, rather slower—or even reversing—when its position weakened; and similarly with the other major industrial countries. Thus we had a very substantial process of adjustment that was unforeseen and unavailable in the "stable state" which the Bretton Woods scheme envisaged.

Since 1960, the opportunities for differential liberalization in international transactions have been much diminished, the process having largely worked itself out before the decade began. In the early 1960's, however, the industrial world, except for the United States, was spared the problem of coping with large imbalances in payments, because the U.S. deficit was so very large, thereby permitting most other countries to remain in balance or even to run large surpluses. And that situation, which arose from the reserve-currency role of the dollar, was also not foreseen in the Bretton Woods system.

Since the mid-1960's, this second development, like the first, has been circumscribed. The United States has been under increasing pressure to cut back its deficit, and we have seen a movement of the world economy back toward restrictions. It represents a reversal of the differential trade liberalization of the 1950's; we now have a differential deliberalization of international payments—first Britain, then the United States, France, and so on. So while the international economy has done spectacularly well, I think it would be a mistake to attribute that to the smooth and effective working of a system of fixed exchange rates. What we have to ask ourselves is: As we look ahead into the next decade, what do we have to substitute for the kinds of mechanisms that were in fact at work—not in principle, in effect—during the past two decades?

In seeking to answer this question, we need to take into account another important postwar development which, like the others I have mentioned, was not foreseen at Bretton Woods. The IMF Agreement, as Eddie Bernstein pointed out, contemplates controls over capital movements. It presupposes a very low degree of capital mobility, whether achieved by controls or by inertia, habit, or other inhibitions. It is a system that is keyed to the current account rather than to all international transactions. Yet one of the really spectacular changes that has taken place in the international economy in the past decade is the tremendous growth in capital mobility. We were treated to the spectacle last November of over $2 billion going into Germany in the course of only three days, in anticipation of an up-valuation of the German mark. This capital mobility is a fact of life which has to be taken into account in any adjustment mechanism of the future. It seems to me that the great weakness of a system of fixed but changeable parities is that it is not really consistent with the kind of freedom of capital movement which we have today despite the controls. And unless conscious efforts are taken to eliminate this weakness, it is going to continue to exist.

Here one should mention the multinational corporation and the role it plays in this speculation. Corporations of course do not like to think of themselves as speculators and, by their own lights, they are not; they simply cover themselves. They must look at financial circumstances and the prospects of financial changes, such as changes in exchange rates, and take whatever protective action they deem necessary. A large part of the funds that move in anticipation of exchange-rate changes are in fact corporations covering their positions. As one looks ahead rather than back, this is likely to be a growing rather than a diminishing problem, and I would plead, in conclusion, that in examining the various alternatives in international adjustment, we take into account these very substantial structural changes that have occurred in the world economy since the Bretton Woods conference of 1944.

Chairman THORP: I think we all want to hear from Frank Southard, who, as a top IMF official, has spent many years dealing with matters of exchange-rate policy.

SOUTHARD: I am inclined to agree with Gottfried Haberler's comment that the Chairman's injunction to ignore political considerations may go a little too far, because one of the important facts of life in international adjustment is a strong *political* resistance to changes in par values. Even in cases where countries have not adopted a par value, there may be strong resistance to changes in the official rate; countries can get just as wedded to an official rate, and find just as much difficulty changing it, as if it were written into the statutes as a par value.

Having said that, I think it is useful to keep in mind that there have been cases in recent years of countries that have worked out a kind of adjustment arrangement which has been successful in overcoming this political difficulty. I will name three, all well documented, that we have worked with in the Fund in just the last couple of years: Chile, Colombia, and Brazil.

In the case of Chile, we have a country that has reconciled itself to a rate of inflation—the figures, by any test, are so big that is doesn't really matter what index one uses—of something around 20 to 30 percent a year. In that country, with its democratic form of government and with its strongly organized trade unions, a high rate of inflation has been accepted as inevitable, and exchange-rate changes are geared very closely to price movements, with anywhere from six to twelve rate changes a year. This, of course, is one way of accommodating to what is fundamentally a rather unsatisfactory internal financial and economic situation.

In the case of Colombia, where there were very strong political hindrances to exchange-rate changes but where the propensity to inflation was not overwhelmingly great, a system was finally worked out providing for small rate changes. That system has worked rather well and has been transitional to a quite successful stabilization effort.

In Brazil, the government has announced that it intends, through rate flexibility, to free itself from political difficulties. While the Brazilian fluctuating rate hasn't been by any means a failure, it has not been as successful, I think, as those in Chile and Colombia.

Thus we have a large number of cases in the less developed world of one or another kind of flexibility. Some have worked quite well, some haven't worked so well, but there are many such cases, right in front of us, all over the world today. But the question which most of us here are concerned with is whether a crawling-peg system could be used successfully by, let's say, the Group of Ten. If a crawling peg won't work for the industrial countries, and particularly if it won't work for the United States, then we need to face that fact and examine the implications.

In this connection, I am impressed with one of the problems emphasized by Dick Cooper a few minutes ago—that is, the extremely large international flows of funds that have occurred during the 1960's. I recall that, prior to the big move to convertibility in the late 1950's, the Fund staff tried to make some guesses of what the potential flows of hot money might be in the new convertible world. I don't want to trust my memory, but I think we came up at one point with a staff judgment that there might be something like $500 million of this kind of money around. It doesn't matter whether the figure was $500 million or $1 billion; the point is that nobody at that time would have dreamed of, or dared to forecast, the kind of float that the world has turned out to have—a float which is manifested in the Eurodollar mass and in other forms as well. How this mass of money can be dealt with and what kind of threat it is to any system, whether a par-value system or a crawling-peg system, is an extremely important problem. This is particularly true if we are thinking in terms of some kind of formula which is supposed to enable a country to adjust its exchange rate gradually to some sensible criteria. If a country's rate under a crawling-peg system is going to have to move as a result of the very substantial impacts arising out of capital flows, what does this do to any concept of overvaluation or undervaluation? Can we really expect that the industrial countries are going to subject themselves to a mandatory system calling for par-value movements, without any way of protecting themselves against influences which they think are transitory, or caused by political factors, or caused by sudden big movements of funds—influences which, in their judgment, are not at all related to the underlying economic realities?

Chairman THORP: Lloyd Metzler would like to explain his case for completely flexible exchange rates.

METZLER: Let me say a few words on why I favor freely fluctuating exchange rates, as opposed to managed flexibility, because there seems to be a good deal of difference of opinion on this issue. A number of economists, among whom

I would include Keynes, have taken a dim view of fluctuating exchange rates, because they have felt that the short-run elasticity of demand for imports is typically so low that a freely fluctuating rate would tend to be highly unstable, shifting up and down in an intolerable way. I don't want to go into a detailed analysis, but what I would call the orthodox theory came to the conclusion that a flexible-rate system would not be stable unless the sum of the demand elasticities were greater than unity. This orthodox notion, however, completely neglected the influence of elasticity of supply. Perhaps the first person to realize this was Sir Roy Harrod in that elegant little book he wrote for the Keynes handbook series. Harrod pointed out that the quantity variable always operated in the right direction, but that a flexible-rate system might be unstable if devaluation had an unfavorable effect on the terms of trade. But we can't come to any conclusions about the terms of trade without examining elasticity of supply. My own conclusion is that while elasticities of demand may be very low in the short run, the short-run elasticities of supply are also likely to be low. This fact has been neglected, and I am firmly convinced that the short-run supply elasticities would tend to stabilize flexible exchange rates.

For these reasons, I agree with Haberler that a system of free-market exchange rates without any impediments would be better than some kind of complicated system. I confess that I did sign a document that appeared in the *New York Times* advocating a crawling peg. I don't particularly like that label, because it sounds too much like a worm, and I was not too happy about signing the document. It was the kind of compromise which one makes with people who believe in flexible exchange rates, on the one hand, and those who believe in fixed rates, on the other. But I had the feeling that if we don't do something, and do it soon, something is going to be done for us. This is not a subject on which we should sit around and have innumerable conferences; we ought to get on with the task of establishing some kind of effective adjustment mechanism. We don't have one now.

HARRIS: I want to say something about the complaint Lloyd Metzler made yesterday regarding the Treasury response to his views on flexible exchange rates. I was chairman of the Treasury consultants on these issues, and I want to tell

Lloyd that he did come out for flexible exchanges at one of our meetings, and so did Gottfried Haberler. I might say that, after one of those meetings, the Secretary of the Treasury as well as the Chairman of the Council of Economic Advisers came to me and said, "We're terribly worried; this thing is going to leak, and everybody will say that Johnson's advisers are for flexible exchange rates. This is going to mean no end of trouble for us." Well, luckily we didn't have a leak, but the point is—as Mr. Silk put it so well—that these issues are more easily decided on economic than on political grounds. I'm sure, for example, that Gardner Ackley was quite friendly to the idea of flexible exchanges, but he certainly couldn't dare to say so, because everybody knew this meant a certain number of votes.

While on this subject, I would like to quote a conversation I once had with Professor Schumpeter at Harvard. I asked him, "Do you really believe that you ought to give your support to flexible exchanges—you who are such a conservative?" And he said, "Well, my dear Seymour, let me tell you that the whole economy is full of rigidities of all kinds everywhere. The only place where you can have any flexibility is in the exchange rate, and that is why I am for flexible exchange rates."

Chairman THORP: There are a number of conferees who are eager to have some discussion of the intermediate solutions which have been suggested—the wider band, the crawling peg, and so forth—and therefore I think we should now move on to explore whether or not these new suggestions seem to us to be sensible. I've asked Fred Bergsten to be a transitional speaker for us—to move us from where we were to where we next ought to be.

BERGSTEN: I would like to start out by taking a bit of exception to what Eddie Bernstein said this morning about the efficacy of the present adjustment process. I think we need to keep firmly in mind the distinction that Sir Roy Harrod made yesterday between dilemma cases of adjustment and nondilemma cases. The nondilemma cases are simply those where external and internal economic requirements call for the same policies.

I think that the cases which Eddie mentioned where adjustment has taken place very nicely—Italy in mid-1960's, Germany a year or two later, and Japan at various times—

have all been of this nondilemma variety, where doing the right thing internally also moves the external position in the right direction. In such cases, there is no conflict in policy and no need for a change in the adjustment rules that prevail. There may be a question of the costs involved; in Italy, some would argue that internal deflation and the cutback in investment went too far, but the basic point I want to make is that there are also dilemma cases, where internal and external economic requirements call for different—or perhaps even opposite—directions of policy.

The United States in the early 1960's is an example; the United Kingdom, it can be argued, has recently been in this category; and Sweden right now is a perfect illustration. And as Sir Roy said yesterday, there is no reason to assume that the dilemma cases are going to be fewer than the nondilemma cases. So I think that what Eddie said has to be modified a bit to recognize that, whereas "good adjustment," as he put it, has taken place, it has been essentially in the nondilemma cases and that in the dilemma cases, where most of the problems lie, we have to look for improvements in the adjustment process.

In examining whether greater exchange-rate flexibility can help in these dilemma cases, I would raise several questions on which we might focus some of our discussion. My first question, which is related to a point made yesterday by Robert Triffin, is this: In dilemma cases, would the improvement in the adjustment process, which we might get from greater exchange-rate flexibility, be greater than the costs in terms of worse adjustment in nondilemma cases, where greater rate flexibility is not needed? This seems to me an important question that we should think carefully about in deciding whether, on balance, greater rate flexibility would improve adjustment in the system as a whole.

A second critical question is whether greater exchange-rate flexibility would contribute toward equalizing the burden of adjustment between the surplus and the deficit countries. Professor Heilperin and others referred to this point yesterday. Under a system of greater rate flexibility, would the burden of adjustment be better shared than it is under the present system? Would the pressures on surplus countries to adjust be greater than they are now?

A third question, which arises when considering limited

exchange-rate flexibility, is whether small but frequent changes in exchange rates—here I'm thinking of the sliding parity—add up to the same adjustment effect over time as one large exchange-rate change, such as we occasionally get under the status quo. For example, the United Kingdom devalued by 14.3 percent in late 1967. Some would contend that, under a sliding parity, the pound would have begun to depreciate as early as 1963. With a crawling peg of 2 or 3 percent a year, would we have had the same new effect as from a 14 percent devaluation after four or more years of holding a rate that was under pressure? I think there are strong arguments on both sides, but the question is important.

A fourth question may be stated as follows: Given the privilege of greater flexibility in the exchange-rate field, how many rates in practice would fluctuate? Would the dollar fluctuate? Would we get adjustment in what I referred to yesterday as the foremost continuing imbalance in the international payments system—the imbalance between the United States and continental Western Europe? Here there are problems on both sides—on the U.S. side, because of the special role of the dollar and, on the European side, because the European Economic Community may be a long way from the time when it will be able to function effectively as a monetary area.

Let me go quickly over the remaining questions that seem to me important. Sir Roy Harrod raised the question yesterday of whether, with flexible exchange rates, the need for international liquidity would be greater or less than under the present system. He thinks the need would be greater; others think it would be much less. Another range of questions concerns the rules of the game under greater exchange-rate flexibility. Specifically, in the case of both the sliding parity and the wider band, should intervention by the monetary authorities be permitted? If so, in what cases, and should it be allowed in the forward market as well as the spot market? Should the wider band or the sliding parity be introduced gradually, or would that risk jeopardizing the success of the whole approach and therefore discredit it? Should the sliding parity, if accepted, be automatic—that is, be governed by some kind of formula—or should it be purely discretionary? And if it is discretionary, how much does it differ from, or how much is it an improvement over, the present system? These are all questions which I think we need to examine if we are to get very far in judging wisely whether greater exchange-rate flexibility would improve the adjustment process.

Chairman THORP: Fred has filled the air with questions. Who is ready to comment? Bob Aliber.

ALIBER: It is Sunday morning, this room looks like a chapel, and I am prepared to make several theological propositions. The first is that the proposal for a wider band is related to only one special aspect of balance-of-payments adjustment—namely, the band's contribution toward dampening capital flows. Discussion of the band really delays consideration of the problem of secular changes in price level relationships. My next theological proposition is that discussion of the sliding parity must come to grips with the institutional question of whether the slide is dictated by formula or by discretion. If the slide is simply the result of discretion, the current system provides for a sliding parity; we need not change the system but only the way countries behave. Thus, we should focus on whether we want to discuss the automaticity of a formula or the role of discretion.

TRIFFIN: I would like to comment briefly on the points raised by Fred Bergsten.

Let me begin with his question: What are the comparative costs of applying wrongly a flexible exchange rate to "nondilemma cases" or of applying wrongly fixed rates to "dilemma cases"? Well, I would say that the obvious answer is that we don't have to apply the wrong remedy in either case. The dilemma, as it is raised, comes primarily from the idea that we have to choose between automaticity and national discretion. But this seems a false choice. I think that national discretion is really impossible, because who will manage the rate? There is only one dollar-sterling rate, not two. If we choose discretion, is the discretion lodged in the Bank of England, or is it lodged in the Federal Reserve? Unless one of the two countries is prepared to surrender sovereignty, we cannot have national discretion. But if we can't have discretion, can we have full automaticity? Here again, I don't believe that this alternative would prove acceptable, which is perhaps the main reason why people who intellectually would like full automaticity resign themselves to national discretion. It seems to me that there is only one third possibility: neither automaticity nor national discretion, but some kind of international consultation—and that is the purpose of my "prong" suggestion.

Mr. Bergsten also raised the question of whether, under greater exchange-rate flexibility, the pressures would be the same for both deficit countries and surplus countries. I would have two comments on that. First, I certainly do believe that, if we retain the concept of discretion, the pressure will always be on the country which is losing reserves, because the depletion of reserves will eventually deprive the deficit country of the ability to support its exchange rate, which will then have to go down. The pressure on the country which is gaining reserves is not of the same order. It can continue to gain reserves, and thus can continue to prevent an appreciation of its rate.

Second, I think that Fred is completely right that the United States is a special case. Its position is asymmetrical. But what does that mean? It means that we must link the adjustment problem with the status of the reserve currencies in the system. Certainly, the adjustment problem of the reserve-currency countries is radically different from that of other countries, because the leverage of the international community on the deficit countries is enormous *except* in the case of the reserve-currency countries. At the same time, there is very little leverage of the international community on the surplus countries, but there is an enormous leverage of the surplus countries on the international community, because they can choose to take their surpluses in gold, in dollars, or in sterling, and they can change their minds tomorrow.

When I speak of leverage, I should add a footnote. The international community can force a country to stop its deficits; if it does not provide the means to finance them, they will stop. But the international community does not have the same leverage to force a country to stop a deficit in the best possible way. That is to say, the country must stop its deficit—it cannot do anything else if it doesn't get the financing—but it remains free to choose between deflation, devaluation, and restrictions.

EXTER: Like Professor Aliber, I find some of this discussion ecclesiastical. I keep thinking how different the world in which I live and think and work is from that in the minds of many around this table. Frank Southard said some of what I wanted to say when he talked about Chile and Colombia. But I think we should first examine how exchange rates are actually determined—what the adjustment process under present monetary arrangements really is.

Most central banks maintain the exchange values of their currencies from day to day by buying and selling dollars, the principal vehicle currency. Even the Bank of England does so, although sterling-area central banks maintain the values of their currencies by buying and selling sterling. The dollar is different, as Henry Wallich has pointed out. The Federal Reserve does not maintain its exchange value by buying and selling foreign currencies, but by buying and selling mostly selling—gold. The Fed must sell gold to maintain the fixed exchange-rate system; if it does not, it (or the Treasury) must borrow. In recent years, the United States has been obliged to borrow heavily: through swaps, through Roosa bonds, through the IMF, or simply through pressing foreign central banks to hold more dollars. As Professor Cooper pointed out a few minutes ago, the German central bank has had to increase its dollar holdings enormously—by $2.5 billion in November alone—and it has "recycled" many more into the Eurodollar market through swaps with its commercial banks. In other words, the German central bank dared not ask us for gold, and so had to lend to the United States by acquiring enormous amounts of dollars over a short period of time, simply to maintain the fixed exchange-rate system.

Why so many dollars? Because of the actions of the illiquid central banks at the top of the pyramid I described yesterday. During November, the Bank of France was creating francs against large amounts of domestic paper assets, francs which the French and others promptly converted into marks. Similarly, the Bank of England was creating sterling against domestic paper assets, sterling which the others also promptly converted into marks. Finally and most important, the Federal Reserve created enormous amounts of dollars against domestic paper assets and foreign-currency assets (resulting from swaps), which Americans and others promptly converted into marks. The Bank of France and the Bank of England defended their currencies by selling dollars, the vehicle currency, to exchange markets, and the German central bank held the mark at its ceiling by buying dollars from the exchange markets. The German central bank bought what gold it could from the Bank of France, but the Bank of France preferred selling dollars. When it and the Bank of England ran out of dollars, they acquired more through swaps with the Federal Reserve Bank of New York, which created hundreds of millions of them against franc and sterling paper assets. The Fed credited them to the Bank of France and the Bank of England, which promptly sold them to exchange markets where they were quickly bought up by the German central bank. That is how the adjustment process actually works, or does not work, in the real world.

The problem of the system cannot be solved through fiddling with the exchange rate any more than a surgeon can cure a cancerous swelling with salve. Our problem is the excessive debt burden in the world. For the United States and the monetary system, it is our inability to pay our debts with $35 gold. We have essentially three choices, and they are gold choices. First, we can maintain the $35 price for gold. To do that, we will have to decelerate our contribution to the growth of the credit pyramid and accept the consequences for the world economy. Second, we can increase the price of gold, which would be a form of debt liquidation but would to some extent improve the liquidity of the system. And third, we can close the gold window. Then we will have a world of floating rates—or, in other words, exchange-rate instability.

Chairman THORP: Thank you, John. It's well to be reminded of the issues you raise, but they get us away from where I think we must concentrate. Fred Bergsten.

BERGSTEN: I'd like to pursue for just a moment which rules would be automatic and which rules would be discretionary. Robert Triffin concluded that there would be problems with both those extremes, so what you need is international consultation. What does that mean? If it means international consultation in which each country still has the sovereign right to determine whether its exchange rate is going to move, then it's really still a discretionary system. If, at the other extreme, it means dictation or final decision-making authority by some international agency, such as the IMF, then I see a massive political problem of getting the system accepted in the first place. We are on the horns of a dilemma; if there is any way we can get between these two choices, maybe we have a viable alternative, but if we can't, then I don't see much improvement over the status quo. I wonder if we can say more about that.

TRIFFIN: I've only one word. I think that it is reasonable to say that countries, within limits, can increase their reserves or reduce their reserves, so to that extent I favor national discretion—but not to the extent where countries impose massive reserve transfers upon others or take a massive amount of reserves from others. At that point, there should be a possibility for the Fund to say to a country: "If you cannot agree on changing the policies which are causing this problem, then you have to accept a flexible rate; you can no longer raid the reserves, or flood the reserves, of other countries." But there would continue to be a wide margin within which national discretion remains. What I reject is full automaticity from the start and under all conditions, because I don't believe that you will ever get it. Even the people who have argued for flexible rates have despaired of the idea of being able to force automaticity. If automaticity can be enforced—and I share Mr. Bergsten's qualms in this respect—it can be enforced more easily *after*, not before, other consultative procedures have failed.

MACHLUP: A word on semantics. Our trouble comes from the word "automatic"; what we are really talking about is action by rule. "Automatic" would mean occurring without deliberate action, or, in the situation we're talking about, it would signify that the central bank does nothing. This is different from action by rule, where a formula tells us what to do.

SOUTHARD: It's hard to find a good word. It is not just a formula; it's a formula which must be automatically used.

MACHLUP: But it's not automatically . . .

SOUTHARD: Well, it's automatic in the sense that if you set up the formula, and if there's a certain movement in the relevant underlying variables, at the end of X weeks or months there must be a change in the par value. That's what we're talking about. I think you've made a good point, but it's not just a matter of formula, because a formula also could be optional.

TRIFFIN: My formula would be national discretion within a wide range, but, beyond that range, it would be international discretion which would then force flexibility.

BERNSTEIN: Mr. Chairman, may I point out that in 1951 the

Fund had a discussion and a paper on fluctuating rates in which this point was very sharply raised. If countries have fluctuating rates and decide, say, to build up their reserves when they have unemployment, this in effect would be using exchange rates on a competitive basis. Therefore, the behavior of reserves is an important criterion in the proper use of a fluctuating system. At the same time, my own experience in Fund negotiations is this: In the end, you cannot impose on countries changes in parities or even a sliding scale; what you can do is give the Fund the opportunity to make representations—reinforced, if you wish, by the Fund using its authority to declare a country ineligible to use its resources. But after the Fund has used its "moral suasion" on the basis of various criteria, including the level of reserves, it is going to have to let the country decide.

SOLOMON: The discussion of the last five minutes reminds me of something I said yesterday—namely, that we do have to think a little about the current-account aims of the countries which are adjusting to each other. One of the things that strikes me about Robert Triffin's very interesting and imaginative suggestion—his "prong" proposal—is that it deals with the over-all balance of payments and not at all with the structure of the balance of payments. I am not being very constructive here, Mr. Chairman; I am just trying to inject another problem for us to think about, but I think the problem may be important. In his very interesting opening remarks yesterday, Fritz Machlup pointed out that Germany has a very large current-account surplus, equal to several percent of its GNP, whereas the United States has a very tiny current-account surplus at the moment, equal to an insignificant percentage of its GNP; and he suggested that there must be a fundamental disequilibrium in this situation. If that is what we mean by a fundamental disequilibrium—some sort of maladjustment in current-account positions—I am not sure that we can content ourselves with Robert Triffin's criterion of reserve changes as a basis for exchange-rate movements. Either we have to abandon Triffin or we have to abandon Machlup.

Chairman THORP: Well, that's very sad. Bob Mundell.

ROBERT A. MUNDELL: I share John Exter's worry that there is something ecclesiastical in the discussion. Of course, everyone has a different model, and one of the symptoms of the enormous complexity of the problem with which we are dealing is the number of different models and visions that people have of the economic system. John Exter has his model, and I understand his model. In fact, I follow him right down to the last "t"—namely, his conclusion.

EXTER: You and I should get together.

MUNDELL: Unlike John, I think that the bottom of his pyramid, in a very fundamental sense, is not gold but the dollar. The dollar is at the bottom of the pyramid, because it is a currency unlike any other; and it makes little sense to speak of widening the exchange margins and introducing a flipping parity, or a yawning parity, or any of these proposed changes, until we talk in terms of the practical cases.

The Security Pacific Bank, one of the conference benefactors, has kindly provided for us a little bit of information which most of you have probably looked at. Among other things, it shows the U.S. economy with a GNP of around $900 billion; then, skipping Russia, it shows, in order, the next four leading countries—Germany, France, Japan, and the United Kingdom—each with a GNP of around $120 billion. In that system, you can't speak of any kind of symmetry, because it is a world in which the U.S. economy dominates.

Paul Samuelson yesterday talked about a dollar problem. For him, the dollar problem is a problem of overvaluation of the dollar. I don't believe that at all. Only, perhaps, with respect to Germany is the dollar overvalued, and, even if this is so, it is not an optimal solution for the United States to change its exchange rate.

Which brings me to the subject of wider bands and crawling pegs. These proposals originated in England, as so many interesting innovations do. Of course I am pro-British, but the British are even more pro-British. The proposed changes in the exchange system are designed—and are perfect—for two countries, Britain and Germany. Why is that? It's because Britain and Germany are the two countries that have not been moving with the main stream of the world economy. Britain has been inflating faster than her growth rate, while Germany has been inflating slower than her growth rate. And so the British economy moves toward deficit, while the German economy moves toward surplus.

For these countries, wider bands and crawling pegs make sense, but we are talking about the problems, not of the whole world, but of two economies.

We already have a good deal of information on how these proposed changes work. Brazil has exactly the system we're talking about. There has been a lot of analysis of the Brazilian experience. Chile has much the same system, and there has been a great deal of study on that. We don't have to have more and more questions perennially asked about how that system operates; we have most of the information. Of course, we can invent a better system than we have now, but the real problem is to begin by understanding what the present system is and how it works—and that system is completely dominated by the dollar. Gold, I would say, has become a sort of constitutional monarch in the system; it simply is not as important as John Exter makes out.

W. RANDOLPH BURGESS: I would like to express very considerable agreement with Professor Mundell. Like him, I think the dollar is the key to the problems we are discussing, and I question whether the United States is a "dilemma case," where our domestic objectives and our international objectives are in conflict. I don't think that is so. As to there being inflation in this country, I can only say that if what we have isn't inflation, I don't know how to recognize it. The resemblance to 1929 is unmistakable. But if we do the things that are required domestically, the dollar will be strong, and we can quit worrying about these little adjustments of exchange rates.

Chairman THORP: Fritz Machlup has something to say on the spreads-and-peg subject.

MACHLUP: I was fascinated with Fred Bergsten's questions about the spot and forward rate, and he has raised several questions in my own mind. A wider band would, of course, apply to the spot rate. Would it be possible to persuade central banks to confine their intervention to the forward market, to which no band limitation applies? Would it be possible for them to do what they want to happen within the band of spot-rate variations by intervening exclusively in the forward market? What would be the effect of that on the forward business of the commercial banks? Would the commercial banks find their risks, their over-all commitments, rising beyond capacity if the total volume of the forward market is thereby enormously increased? Is the so-called limit of capacity in the forward market really a limit, or does it merely reflect the fact that some banks are very traditional and believe they cannot possibly handle twice as much business as they do now?

HARROD: Might I say, as regards Machlup's main question, that intervention confined to the forward market may be feasible, but you've got to be sure that there are enough arbitrage funds, because the spot rate has to be kept within the band, and you won't keep it within the band in the spot market unless there are enough arbitrage funds to do that in the forward market. We've often had the experience that there just weren't enough arbitrage funds to keep the two rates in line. Where this is true, forward intervention would be of no avail.

On another point, I contend that absolutely freely floating rates would give us intolerable oscillations. I refer in particular to seasonal, cyclical, and random variations in the balance of supply and demand. We have deficits arising for those three reasons. They may add up to something rather big. We may have quite large random movements caused, for instance, by an important strike or by an obviously supernormal capital flow at one particular time. If there's no official intervention—and that's what we mean by freely floating rates—there's bound to be undesirable oscillation even if the private people have infinite knowledge of what is to happen.

MACHLUP: But against whom in this room are you arguing? Nobody around this table has argued that we should have freely fluctuating exchange rates.

HARROD: Well, wait a moment. Is that so? If it's not worth talking about freely floating rates, I'll stop talking about them. I didn't know there was this consensus.

Chairman THORP: No, I think Fritz is wrong here. After all, we have Lloyd Metzler and, at least in the world outside, he is not alone.

MACHLUP: I apologize to Sir Roy.

HARROD: I'll say one more word about the freely floating rate. If you have a freely floating rate, those who advise business on the movement of funds, even if they are perfectly correct in their views, will not advise the purchase of a fluctuating currency unless they think the rate will rise—which means they think the rate is below its equilibrium level. How far the rate has to go down one doesn't know. On top of that, of course, I don't think these advisers are infinitely wise; I've watched them very closely during the vagaries of sterling in the last few years, and they seem to be very strange people. I'm thinking not only of times when there was a sudden loss of confidence in sterling for no good reason but of times when there was a sudden upsurge of confidence in sterling for no good reason. When I discovered the explanation for the shift in confidence, it was usually an absolutely ridiculous reason.

Let me say a few words about the managed flexible rate. With a managed rate, the authorities must use reserves to reduce the excessive oscillations caused by seasonal, cyclical, and random fluctuations. Under the fixed-rate system, private capital normally supplies the funds needed to deal with these three things, because, when the rate is near the lower limit, the currency becomes absolutely cheap and therefore the business advisers say, "Buy now, buy now." With a floating rate, there is no absolute cheapness or absolute dearness and, to avoid intolerable oscillations, the authorities must intervene, because private capital will not do the job. That means that the authorities must have bigger reserves than they are required to have under a fixed rate. The British experience was perfectly clear during our floating-rate period from 1931 to 1939; we had to have and to use much bigger reserves than we ever had to have under a fixed-rate system.

Now I come to the crawling peg, on which we have had some semantic discussion. What I mean by a crawling peg is that the parity moves downward or upward according to a formula. Of course, the authorities have to intervene at the margins, because there are margins on either side of parity, but the parity itself is moving. With a crawling peg, the reserves required would not be quite so great as with a managed flexible rate, because when the currency was at the bottom of the band there would be helpful private movements of capital—not to the same extent as with a fixed rate, but to some extent.

All of this has nothing to do with major breaks of confidence. That is quite another thing. Of course, the worst system for breaks in confidence is undoubtedly the present system of the adjustable peg. You could have a break in confidence under the crawling peg, but it would lead to less movement of funds. Under the present system, we try to shield ourselves from disaster with these widely acclaimed swap arrangements. Mr. Bernstein referred to them in a way I am not entirely happy about. He said that the resources of the Fund were sufficient, though he might want to raise them a little. He added that we have vast resources outside the Fund—referring, of course, to the swap arrangements. I would point out, however, that there is an understood division of labor whereby these resources outside, which can be galvanized through swaps, are designated for the purpose of forestalling breaks in confidence. They are not intended to finance deficits. To see what the world system is providing for financing deficits, we have to look at the resources of the Fund.

One final point. I'm British—I think I'm the only non-North American around the table—so I should be very diffident in what I say. On the other hand, perhaps being the only non-American imposes a responsibility on me. In any case, I think there's a great illusion about the dollar being in a different position as regards the possibility of devaluation. I would say there is no difference in kind; there may be a difference in degree, which occurs because the United States is by far the most important country.

But there are other important countries too. Any important country must have some restraint; it can't just do what it likes in the way of devaluation. The United States is under great restraint, because if it devalues its currency, other countries are likely to follow suit. It is sometimes said that all other countries would follow suit, but that isn't necessarily so. If there was a consensus among other countries that the dollar was overvalued, there could perfectly well be agreement that, if the United States devalued, the others would not, or only some would. It's a question of agreement. But what I want to stress is that this situation is not peculiar to the dollar; it applies to other importance currencies.

For example, the United Kingdom hasn't the power to do just what it likes; it has to get a consenus. Take the 1949 devaluation. We devalued, but more than half the world devalued too. Thus, for us, the devaluation was largely frustrating. A much more striking example of lack of freedom is our devaluation of 1967. The United Kingdom was subject to very powerful constraints then as regards the amount of devaluation.

Now, I'll reveal my own preference; I'm not in sympathy with those who think we ought to have devalued earlier. On the whole, I think it was right not to. But there are a lot of people who think that we ought to have devalued more. We *could not* devalue more. We were like the United States; we could devalue by the amount we did, because there was a consensus among the relevant people that the poor old British had been laboring under an overvalued pound and should be permitted to devalue a bit—but not by more than we actually did. We were inhibited from going beyond 14.3 percent because of the threat that, if we went beyond that, a lot of countries would devalue with us. The devaluation was supported by very large credits, and it is very doubtful that we could have obtained those credits if we had proposed to go beyond 14.3 percent. So we were subject to very severe constraints. I hope I have made my point plain.

Chairman THORP: I think that your point is absolutely clear. Arthur Young.

ARTHUR N. YOUNG: I would like to call attention to two or three lessons which may be useful in connection with suggestions that there should be management of exchange rates and that rates should be flexible.

First, I am wholeheartedly in agreement with the idea that permitting rates to fluctuate widely is justifiable only in very exceptional circumstances, and leads to all the difficulties that Sir Roy has so clearly stated. I hope we all agree on that.

Attempts to manage fluctuating rates are in a different category, but there are some very real difficulties there. In China, we attempted to "check undue fluctuations." We found that this requires very great judgment, trying to determine when to intervene and by how much; and it requires, of course, centralized decision-making. It requires also the utmost integrity of those who are making the decisions, as there is always a very real risk that rate managers will be tempted to profit by their own operations. And even an honest manager is likely to be charged with trying to make personal profits, with favoritism, and with the neglect of certain important economic interests in the community.

Another lesson is that when rates are managed, they tend in practice to become pegged. Moreover, there is a strong bias in such pegging in favor of overvaluation. It is very hard to get away from an overvalued rate, because the exchange rate, especially in a weak or a deteriorating situation, is viewed as a measure of the strength of the government, and there is a very strong resistance to moving it to a realistic level. I was glad to hear Frank Southard say that in several of the South American countries there has been a growing sophistication in this field. I think we must work for that, but as a practical matter there is this feeling—and not only in the less developed countries—that depreciation in exchange, even when it is clearly called for, is a serious blow that is not only going to raise import prices but is going to cause a loss of confidence.

In conclusion, I think that managed rates tend to impede trade and to lead to trade restriction because of their tendency to result in overvaluation. I strongly hope that fluctuating rates will be viewed as a temporary and emergency matter, and I think that the Fund, as Frank Southard and Eddie Bernstein have shown, affords great flexibility under the present arrangements.

PATTERSON: A question raised by Fred Bergsten which I find interesting is whether a series of small changes in exchange rates would have the same effect as one large change. I don't pretend to know the answer, but Bob Mundell said that we know enough already and that all we need to do is to draw some conclusions. I wonder whether his work on the Brazilian, Chilean, and other cases provides an answer to this question. Are the effects of a series of small changes the same as those of one large change in the rate? Or are there great differences? If so, is the big difference the difference in the response of wage rates?

MUNDELL: I think the fundamental difference is with respect to expectations. A series of small devaluations, when a currency is overvalued, results in a situation where the expected future of the currency is lower. This has a persistent effect on the forward market which, in turn, has an effect on interest rates. Take Britain, for instance. If the British had devalued by 30 percent instead of by 14 percent, British interest rates would now be, not 8 percent, but 6 percent or 5 percent. Or take Germany. The undervaluation of the mark—the belief in the mark's undervaluation—means that German interest rates over the past three years have come down from 9½ percent in 1966 to about 5 percent at the present time. This is very directly a reflection of expectations. Thus there is a fundamental difference between a big change in the exchange rate and a series of little changes; the two situations are poles apart.

BERNSTEIN: I think, Bob, that if you have a system of gradually moving parities—moving, say, by 1 or 2 percent a year—you will not necessarily destroy the expectation that occasionally a large rate change will be needed, which means that you may get all the troubles that you have mentioned. The sliding peg is presumably most useful for the very thing that Paul Samuelson stressed yesterday—namely, structural changes. Changes in the real economic position of a country do tend to take place slowly. A 1 or 2 percent per year change in parity would take care of that problem; but unless you destroy the expectation of large rate changes, you haven't avoided the difficulties that you have described.

On another point, I would not want to leave the impression that the Fund was unaware of dilemma cases. The Fund Agreement recognized that there are dilemma cases; that's why it provided for changes in parity. But I would like to emphasize that I know of no dilemma cases, not a single one, in which excessive aggregate demand at some stage was not an element in creating the dilemma. And I would add that dilemma cases can occur even with fluctuating rates. Countries will have to stop the excessive demand or the fluctuating-rate system won't work.

ALEXANDER: I thought the dilemma case was the case where you didn't have excess demand but did have a price rise.

BERNSTEIN: Well, what I said was this: In a country which has an exchange rate which is not suitable . . .

ALEXANDER: But not suitable for which reason? May I just take a minute? There is great importance in the distinction that I thought Bergsten made—the distinction between an essentially cost-push situation, with no excess aggregate demand, which is the dilemma case, and a situation of excess aggregate demand and external deficit, which is the nondilemma case. In the nondilemma case, the solution is clear, however difficult it may be.

BERNSTEIN: Well, the dilemma case that I have in mind is the following: Here is a country which is no longer generating additional excess demand but which has a balance-of-payments deficit. If it tries to restore equilibrium at the present rate of exchange, it will have unemployment. My point is that this dilemma case in every instance I know—in fact, I can think of no exceptions—is the result of an earlier situation of excessive demand which had altered the relationships of prices and costs in such a way as to make impossible the correction of the balance of payments at the existing exhange rate without causing a depression. And I would add my second proposition, which is that if a country isn't going to control excess demand, fluctuating rates aren't going to help much.

SILK: I'm sure it's much too early—say, five years too early—for any kind of consensus to emerge, but as one who does not regard himself as a great technician in the exchange-rate field, I wonder whether I might nevertheless make an observation or two.

In particular, it seems to me a mistake to set up all our alternatives on an either-or basis. As one looks at each of the various exchange-rate proposals, one may well find quite serious objections to any particular proposal being the *sole* route one follows to achieve greater adjustment flexibility, and I think we should bear in mind that we may want to pursue several approaches at the same time—provided, of course, that they are mutually consistent.

Certainly, in the short run and in the normal course of events, many people who have different ideological positions can see some virtues in a fixed-rate system. From the standpoint of the banks, the central banks, and the business community, there are very real advantages; and as a kind of normal state, under fair-weather conditions, there are no powerful objections to having pegged rates. They force adjustments to be made.

At the same time, slow changes do occur in the structure of the system and in the structure of particular economies. These changes call, not for abrupt, but for gradual changes in the pattern of exchange rates. Such adjustments might best be achieved by a sliding, or crawling-peg, system if the technicians could figure out a nondisturbing way to get that. One can argue, of course, that small changes might not do a great deal of good in the short run, but neither would they do much harm, and over time they would avoid the necessity for enormously destabilizing changes in rates or shifts from currencies.

There may be occasions, however, where the crawling peg may not provide all the flexibility that is needed. This leads me to the third element in my thinking, which focuses on the need for more effective international consultation. In this area, improvement is needed and is possible. Such improvement perhaps can best be achieved by the IMF writing for itself a new set, not of rules, but of guidelines for its interventions. To sum up, my prescription would consist of three elements: fixed exchange rates in the short run, gliding adjustments over time which are nondisturbing, and a better procedure for negotiating major exchange-rate changes—a procedure which assures that such changes occur before, rather than after, an international crisis.

SALANT: The points I want to make are all related to the question of whether we may be overlooking some difficulties associated with adjustment under flexible exchange rates. We are all so keenly aware of the difficulties under fixed exchange rates—because we have experienced them—that we naturally ask ourselves whether those same difficulties would exist under flexible rates. If we find that they do not, but fail to ask whether any new difficulties arise, we are in danger of concluding that the case for flexible rates is stronger than it may actually be.

Under a flexible-rate system, as we all know, the adjustment in the deficit country has to be very largely an internal adjustment, involving shifts in the direction of domestic demand. By raising the price level in domestic currency of imports and of exportable goods, a fall in the exchange value of the deficit country's currency encourages a shift in its demand toward domestic goods away from tradeable goods, thereby tending to improve its trade balance both by discouraging imports and by encouraging exports. As Randall Hinshaw pointed out in an article several years ago, it is much easier to get this kind of shift, which is necessary in any case, through a fall in the exchange value of the currency than under a fixed-rate system, because adjustment in the latter case requires a fall in the price level of domestic goods—both absolutely and in relation to the price level of tradeable goods.

The point I want to make is that, while it is true that a fall in the exchange value of its currency eases adjustment for the deficit country, the difficulties which confront the deficit country under a fixed-rate system are, in effect, transferred to the surplus country under a flexible-rate system. The surplus country undergoes a fall in its price level induced by a fall in the prices of import and export goods—that is, it experiences precisely the same pressures that the deficit country resists under fixed exchange rates. I doubt that we can blithely assume that surplus countries will not resist that pressure. The German resistance to upward revaluation of the mark supports my doubt. Of course, one may say that the surplus country with a mortal fear of inflation does not have the problem of price rises under a flexible-rate system. But the deficit country then *does* have that problem. In other words, what I am trying to make clear is that some of the main difficulties that people have worried about in connection with a fixed-rate system do not disappear under a flexible-rate system; they are simply transferred, the difficulties of the deficit countries appearing in the surplus countries.

One more point. To the extent that the demands of the various claimants on real income are excessive, the adjustment problem for a deficit country is not just a monetary problem. If an inflation is a reflection of claims on the national product which add up to more than the economy can supply, no exchange-rate system is going to remedy that. It is not a monetary problem, and the fact is that we do not know the extent to which our difficulties are of that kind.

CHAPTER V

DIALOGUE ON THE OPTIONS: OTHER CHOICES

This chapter is a scenario of the third and final day of the Claremont conference. As agreed earlier, the day was assigned to a discussion of alternatives in international adjustment outside the realm of exchange-rate policy, but members were encouraged to develop any points on other matters that they felt had received insufficient attention.

R. H.

Chairman THORP: We have one considerable area yet to cover, and that is the general problem of dealing with a payments disequilibrium by taking action at some point in the economy other than by adjusting exchange rates.

The immediate postwar practice was to deal with a deficit through quotas on imports. You may remember the instance in which the United Kingdom and other sterling-area countries cut back their imports by 25 percent as a way of restoring balance. At the moment, we in the United States have certain very specific controls intended to improve the situation, particularly in the field of capital. There has also been talk about doing something in the field of travel—and some things have been done, as those of us know who have tried to bring products into the United States from other places in the last few months.

We need to examine such possibilities outside the field of exchange-rate policy, the topic we discussed yesterday. Border taxes have already been mentioned several times, and there may be more we wish to say about fiscal and monetary policy, since some of our group believe that inflation is the great devil in the picture. In order that we may leave the meeting with a minimum of frustration, I propose that we open the discussion today to whatever phases of our conference theme that we feel need to be further emphasized. We shall begin with an economist who, although much in evidence as our host, has not yet performed as an economist, Randall Hinshaw.

RANDALL HINSHAW: My remarks are intended to link the discussion of yesterday with the discussion of today.

I think that John Exter, whom I've known and admired for many years, is one of the heroes of this conference—not because we all agree with his conclusions, but because, with his earnest manner of strong conviction, he makes us think more carefully, and perhaps more nervously, about our own conclusions. In particular, I find his model of an inverted pyramid most disturbing. It is hard to imagine a more unstable equilibrium than a pyramid balanced on its apex. For his own peace of mind as well as for ours, I wish that John could be persuaded to think of his pyramid as right side up.

Which end is up, however, is only one question. Another question is what is at the tip of the pyramid, whether down or up. Is it gold, as John thinks, or it is dollars, as Bob Mundell maintains? I can think of a test—which I am not at the moment proposing—that might give us the answer. The test would be for the U.S. Treasury to stop selling gold to, or buying gold from, foreign monetary authorities. What would happen? The two dollar prices for gold, the private and the official, would become a single price, and conceivably that price might rise to a level well above $35 an ounce.

But that would not prove anything very interesting. The important thing is what would happen to the dollar prices of the major foreign currencies. Would these currencies remain pegged to the dollar at their present parities, or would they appreciate? This question would undoubtedly cause much furrowing of brows in continental surplus countries, such as Germany. If these countries were to appreciate their currencies, their competitive position in relation to the United States—and in relation to those countries which did not follow suit—would deteriorate, and they would hear loud cries of protest from their exporters. If they maintained their present parities, they would have to accept settlement for their surpluses in dollars which they could no longer exchange for gold at bargain prices, and they would remain confronted with a major source of inflationary pressure. My guess is that some of the surplus countries would appreciate—a little.

But so what? This would mean only that the dollar price of a Volkswagen might be a little higher or that the cost of a trip to Europe would be a little more. This would make far more sense, in my opinion, than telling Americans not to buy Volkswagens, or telling them not to go to Europe, or slapping on import taxes or quotas, or doing a lot of other dubious things that have been advocated in high places. In this connection, I think we have already learned something from the alteration in gold policy worked out almost a year ago. In late 1967 and in early 1968, particularly after the dreary proposals of President Johnson on New Year's Day, it was not difficult to reach the conclusion that mankind once more was in danger of being crucified on a cross of gold. The two-price gold agreement, whatever else can be said about it, separated our real economic problems from some of our basically phony ones. It showed that, unless we insist, gold need be neither at the apex of Exter's pyramid nor the master of our destiny.

I would like to conclude with one more comment. It has been said that there are certain economists who have an almost theological opposition to import taxes, quotas, tariffs, and other methods of limiting imports. If that charge is meant to include me, I plead guilty. While I'm not very happy with the metaphor, I would say that if the conviction that our salvation does not lie in import barriers is to be labelled theology, then we need a return to religion.

HOWARD S. ELLIS: I promised the Chairman to keep my animadversions within a band of five to ten minutes; please be reassured.

The proposition that I would like to make and defend is that a discussion of the adjustment mechanism ought to have some reference to what we are adjusting to, and within what kind of system we are adjusting. By this I mean, specifically, whether we are on a dollar standard, or something like a Triffin arrangement, or a Bernstein system, or a real international money, such as the Special Drawing Rights, which are actually to be created by international authority, *and managed.* I believe that most of the things that have been said about adjustment would be applicable in almost any system, but certainly it makes some difference what we have for reserves and what kind of a system we are operating in. It is this theme that I would like to embroider a bit.

I am going to omit the gold standard because, despite my near neighbor, John Exter, and my great esteem for him, I consider the gold standard as dead as a dodo; I think it has been dead since the guns of August 1914, since which it has only twitched. The parities of the Fund in gold are certainly just nominal, and the real causation runs from the dollar to gold; the dollar determines the value of gold, not the other way around. So the dollar is the standard, even though gold is used as one form of reserves and settlement. I am therefore barring the gold standard from discussion, though I may return to it briefly.

I would also like to remark that I think the dollar standard is not going to last forever. It has often been said that we cannot expect the United States to supply the international currency, because the dollar, as an international currency, has a fatal propensity for killing itself off. The more popular it gets and the bigger the superstructure of credit, the more apt people are to distrust it and make runs. It's self-destructive. I think that this is the phenomenon which John Exter has in mind when he fears some kind of a crash.

We are now rather rapidly on our way to some alternative international currency arrangement. Indeed, I think we should be. So far as concerns gold, the events of last March certainly amounted almost to a demonetization. I welcome this change, and I would join Professor Hansen in suggesting ways to get rid of the gold before the bottom drops out of its value. I would satisfy our creditors just the way they like, sell the stuff while it's good, and perhaps also get a little bit of what the Austrians call *Schadenfreude*—that is, triumphant glee in the downfall of one's opponent.

Of course, even if gold were completely demonetized, there still would be speculation in the international markets as between currencies—dollars against pounds, marks against francs, and so on. For this reason, I would welcome some approach to a real international money. There is an additional reason, mentioned by Leonard Silk, for wishing that the dollar standard would not persist, and that is that the Europeans certainly resent the situation. I agree with others around the table who feel that political realities such as this ought not to be neglected completely. And I certainly feel that managing an international standard is too much of a responsibility for this country alone.

Now a few words about flexible exchange rates, but in a mild way. I don't want to advocate freely fluctuating exchange rates, but I think we are bound to progress in the direction of having more adjustment by this route. And I don't feel like taking *no* for an answer. If it is said that all the bankers and all the congressmen are opposed to flexible rates, that is no answer—just as it was no answer, thirty years ago, to use the same arguments against deficit financing during a time of depression.

On the issue of flexibility, I do not see why countries should not, within some considerable range, decide whether they want to have a fixed rate or a variable rate. In some measure, they do decide now; why not increase this freedom? I suppose that the key countries would want to have a pretty stable rate and would not change their exchanges very often. This could all be operated within the mechanism of the Fund, as it is supposed to be.

In my mind, these two subjects—the gold standard and the fixed exchange rate—go together. Between them, they were the chief authors of a nefarious national monetary illusion—the illusion that if you had the dignities and the alleged immunities of a gold standard and of a fixed exchange rate, you were in good company, you were respectable. And this mentality, I think, caused a great deal of damage. With the disappearance of the remnants of the gold standard, and with greater exchange flexibility, the way should be cleared toward better arrangements.

I regard the Triffin Plan and the Bernstein Plan as very promising indeed. They are on the way to international money. They are not international money themselves exactly, because true international money should not only be managed by an International Monetary Fund, or something like it, but should be created by it. Therefore, I regard the Special Drawing Rights as the scriptural "cloud the size of a man's hand" which shows what kind of money we are going to have and ought to have.

One more word, before I stop, about the character of an international monetary authority. Such an authority, whether the IMF or any alternative, should evolve and apply rules, and it should use discretion too. It should use both rules and discretion to determine how much discretion is to be left to national authorities. I want to emphasize particularly the power of the banker's sanction of being able to decline to lend. An international monetary system is very much more precarious than a national system, and therefore it needs to grasp any power that it has and to use it. In a national system, factor mobility is practically perfect. Moreover, there are no competing creators of money; there are near-moneys, of course, but money is a monopoly of the state. It is quite otherwise in the international system. Hence any power that the international monetary authority has should be exploited, including the power to decline to lend if a country is behaving badly from an international point of view. Now the statutes of the Fund state very explicitly that the Fund shall not interfere with the domestic affairs of its members, and this is all right. But this does not imply that we shouldn't have rules and try to enforce them. I don't think that a banker who says to a loan applicant, "Well, I'm sorry, but after reviewing your situation, I'm not going to lend to you," is interfering with the applicant's private affairs.

All this is perhaps way off in the wild blue yonder, but I do see a few more or less immediate implications. I would very much hope that the Special Drawing Rights, as soon as their use has been sanctioned and established, could be made available on some other basis than just a flat quota system. I think they ought to be reserves to be used at the discretion of the international authority, and this is one of the reasons I have emphasized the importance of the banker's sanction in creating rules and precedents. As a matter of fact, all the Fund's assets should partake of this character eventually, and then we really would have international money. As another immediate implication, we ought to have a review of the character of our international monetary authority—to examine, among other things, whether the Fund, composed of 110 or 115 countries, should not be a sort of debating society and legislative authority, with another distinct executive authority composed of central bankers, who have been praised, I think quite rightly, by one of our speakers.

BERNSTEIN: Mr. Chairman, I want to make a very slight correction in what Professor Ellis said. The statutes of the Fund state that when a country comes in to request a change in parity, the Fund shall not deny that change in parity on account of the country's domestic policies. The Fund does have the absolute authority to refuse to allow drawings on its resources, even within quota limits, when a country is not using the resources to carry out the purposes of the Fund. In fact, it has the authority to suspend completely a country's drawing privileges. Except for the gold tranche, there is no automaticity, no absolute right, to get the resources of the Fund.

ELLIS: I certainly welcome this more precise statement.

Chairman THORP: I think perhaps we might see if there is further discussion of the points raised by Mr. Ellis. Bob Mundell.

MUNDELL: I would like to go on from where Professor Ellis led us in his remarks. Whatever we call it, we are now on a dollar standard, in effect, though with a gold-leaf covering to it. The problem is that the Federal Reserve System is running it, and I think we would all agree that in the past three years it has not been running it very well. That is because, during a wartime period, our goals get mixed up. In any case, we have been inflating too rapidly. I suppose the dollar standard would be more compatible with the interests of other countries if it were run better—in particular, if the inflation, the growth of prices in the world economy, were slowed down. But in the long run, I don't think that a dollar standard is going to be accepted by the other countries of the world, and the emergence of a dollar bloc, which would be a narrowing of that standard, could conceivably be accompanied by the emergence of a gold bloc in Europe. This would be a two-bloc system, one based on gold and one based on the dollar. We don't know about that; probably, over the next five years, we will have some kind of transitional system, in which the dollar standard will still be the dominant element.

But I am disturbed by the fact that we haven't changed intellectually with the change in the world. The world that Keynes was writing about when he was supporting flexible exchange rates was a far different world from the one we have today. It was a world, in the 1920's, of middle-sized states. There was no great superpower. That situation has changed in a way which makes the adjustment problem fundamentally different. The arguments for flexible exchange rates, which were valid in the world of the 1920's, are not valid in the world of today.

Even more important than the revolution in the relative sizes of states is the revolution in communication. In earlier years, a flexible exchange system was regarded as preferable to a fixed-rate system because of rigidities in the economy and, in particular, because of the money illusion. But money illusion, in a world of accelerating communication, no longer amounts to much. It is too temporary. Earlier, a country could ordinarily gain by devaluing, as it took three or four or five years for the workers to discover that their real wages had been cut. This period has now been reduced to a few months.

Take the French case. If workers in France insist on excessive wage increases, and if their demands are met, then devaluation, it is said, will be necessary. But devaluation, of course, would cancel out the bulk of the gain from the increase in wages, which could lead to new wage demands and further devaluation. This means that our intellectural arguments have to go deeper than simply saying that we need flexible exchange rates. We may need to move, in other words, toward a system in which we have a band or a sliding parity, but the band or the sliding parity may have to be around wage rates.

PATTERSON: The Chairman has asked us to look at adjustment measures outside the exchange-rate field, but it appears almost ungracious to do so, since our host began this morning by implying that if one wanted to condone variations in trade restriction as an adjustment mechanism, one was really very much against the angels. Nevertheless, it seems to me that for us to talk about adjustment policies and not grapple with the subject of changes in trade restraints is simply to fail to deal with what in fact has been a major aspect of the adjustment process for the past twenty years. And if Bob Mundell is right in asserting that even a wider band is not going to work well, or if we continue to have important dilemma cases of the sort Fred Bergsten has talked about, then it is clear to me that variations in trade restriction will continue to be an important method of adjustment. Of course the method is messy and involves the danger of serving the cause of protection. But nothing is gained by ignoring it. To try to improve this approach does not mean that we give the approach our blessing; it is simply a matter of trying to minimize the damage of what countries have been doing, and will continue to do, whether we like it or not.

MUNDELL: Washington has a real information problem. It has had great difficulty, in the past eight years, acquiring a view of the system that has increasingly been agreed to by most modern scientists—the view that the balance-of-payments devices imposed by the United States have not effectively corrected or helped our payments position. Empirically, that has been established, as established as anything could be. And quite apart from this, of course, we know from economic theory that these devices are bad. But the information problem remains of teaching some common sense to the economists who are in Washington and who are making U.S. government policy.

BERGSTEN: After Mundell's rabble-rousing call to arms against the gnomes of Washington, I don't know how I should respond. But I do think one ought to answer Bob at least to the following extent. Everybody agrees that the surpluses that were shown on the two official definitions of the U.S. payments position last year were really transitory and did not reflect any lasting equilibrium. Nevertheless, one must admit that the controls on direct investment abroad did have an important impact in shifting the source of financing such investment, and therefore had a major impact on our payments position in the short run. One can argue whether this was good or bad, but I think it is a fact, and to say that the controls had no effect is a mistake.

But let me go on to ask two questions inspired by Gardner Patterson's remarks about controls. The first question is: Do we as economists, perhaps not liking any form of control, have a sharp preference between controls which operate on trade (or, more broadly, on the current account) and controls which operate on the capital account? I think there is a real choice here. The U.S. government has taken measures that focus on the capital account rather than on the current account, although there were some noises in the latter direction a year ago. Nevertheless, the primary emphasis has been in the capital-account sector. Query: From an economic standpoint, is that correct? We have already heard a yes and a no, so that might be a good question to pursue.

My second question is: Do we as economists prefer market-oriented controls of the interest-equalization tax type or do we prefer administrative controls? Perhaps that question is sharpest in the trade area, where one has an option in practice between quantitative restrictions and import surcharges. I think these are two fruitful questions to pursue as economists, recognizing, as Gardner Patterson did, that these measures have been, and no doubt will continue to be, used as part of the adjustment process. And I think that economists, no matter how they may dislike this grubby type of adjustment measure, are really derelict in their responsibilities if they don't help those who have a role in operating this machinery to answer those questions.

Chairman THORP: I now have several applications for the floor. The first I saw signal is Eddie Bernstein.

BERNSTEIN: A few months ago, Fritz Machlup made a very interesting observation at a meeting of the Treasury consultants on controls. What he said was that controls don't work, and he then went on to explain what I would call the Machlup adaptation of Say's Law to controls. Controls don't work, Fritz said, because if you put on controls, other countries will have less receipts and therefore will spend less abroad; in other words, a reduction in your foreign outlays will result in a reduction in your foreign receipts.

Now this version of Say's Law, applied to international economics, is not strictly correct. Say's Law may not even be correct when applied to the domestic economy, but it definitely isn't right when applied to the international sector because countries have the option of holding reserves or drawing on reserves. It also isn't right because the country that imposes the controls is not the only country on which any reduction in expenditure by the countries losing receipts may fall.

Instead of Say's Law, I would propose as a more adequate theory what I would call Keynes's Law of international payments. Keynes's Law says essentially the following: In every country, the balance of payments on current account will be equal to the domestic savings of the community minus its home investment. Assuming no change in demand conditions abroad, this means that when a country has an unfavorable change in its current-account position, it is because the country has increased its spending either on investment or on consumption (which will have reduced domestic saving), and a part of the increased expenditure will spill over into the balance of payments.

Applying this analysis to controls, I would conclude that controls on capital will be effective in reducing an over-all payments deficit, but I would not have the same view about controls on imports. Let me explain why. Consider a country like the United Kingdom that puts a 15 percent surcharge on imports without doing anything to curb domestic consumption or investment. In such a situation, what does the surcharge do? It makes imports a little more expensive relative to home goods. This means that the community, still having too much to spend, will shift some of its spending from imports to home goods, including export goods. I don't say that an import surcharge has a zero effect on the balance of payments; I merely say that, unless accompanied by measures to restrict aggregate expenditure, the effect will be largely dissipated. If controls on imports are to be effective in reducing a payments deficit, they must be accompanied by measures to restrain aggregate demand.

This is not true of capital controls. To be effective, capital controls do not require the same sort of demand restraint as import controls. The demand restraint is still a good idea, since it is excessive demand that makes any form of control needed, but in the absence of such restraint, capital controls will be more effective than import controls.

Let me conclude with two or three sentences which summarize my philosophy. I don't like these controls. I do believe that there may be cases in which they are justified. But I believe that most of them would be unnecessary, and in any case would be more effective, if they were accompanied by proper policies affecting aggregate demand and the availability of money in the national economy.

Chairman THORP: The Chairman has denied Professor Machlup the opportunity to expound further the Machlup interpretation of Say's Law, and therefore gives the floor to Gottfried Haberler.

HABERLER: I want to start out by trying to give a concrete answer to the question: If we are confronted with a choice between capital controls and trade controls, which would we choose? I am not going into such complicated matters as Say's Law to support my answer. I agree with Eddie Bernstein that, if proper policies are pursued, neither type of control should be necessary, but let us assume that we are in a situation where we have to make such a choice. In that event, I would prefer capital controls to trade controls for the pragmatic reason that trade controls are more likely to work very well and can be more easily evaded. But even if they do work well, capital controls become so obnoxious after a while that they are likely to be eliminated, whereas trade controls are very difficult to get rid of because of the growth of vested interests.

But I would hope that we need not make that choice, and I would like to go back to the important question raised by Randall Hinshaw. Randall started out by asking what would happen if the dollar were declared inconvertible into gold. I think he meant that as a measure of last resort; he would agree, I am sure, that we should first do other things. But if the other things don't work, it is important to keep in mind that we have this measure of last resort. I fully agree with Professor Hinshaw that if we are unable to persuade others to adopt more flexible exchange rates or if we are unable to curb inflation sufficiently, we need not make a choice between capital controls and trade controls, as we have a much better alternative—namely, in such a situation, to declare the dollar inconvertible into gold.

Nothing terrible would happen. Most countries would doubtless continue to peg to the dollar. Two or three countries in a strong surplus position would have to make a choice, and I would be very happy to let them make that choice—whether to peg to the dollar, or peg to gold, or float, or appreciate, or whatever they wish. In any case, it is extremely important to know that we always have a good way out and that nobody can force us either to impose obnoxious controls or to deflate and have more unemployment than is needed to stop inflation. And I sometimes have the feeling that our negotiators are not aware that they have this alternative.

Now I come to Howard Ellis, who tells us that gold is out or is on the way out. Maybe so; I fully agree that the gold standard, in any real sense, is dead, and I agree that gold *may* be on the way out, but I think it will take quite some time. Howard then talked about the various plans—the Triffin Plan, the Bernstein Plan, the Machlup Plan, the Mundell Plan, and so on—and he endorsed them all. I think they are all worth discussing, but I would like to raise one question. These plans presuppose that there must be some harmonization of policies, at least in the monetary and fiscal field. Without such harmonization, I really don't see how any of these plans can work better than the present system. Of course, one can imagine that an international agency simply creates enough international money to accommodate the most inflationary member of the group, but that would not be acceptable to the less inflationary members.

If you ask me whether we are ready to have the necessary harmonization of national monetary and fiscal policies, my answer is definitely no. We may be moving in that direction; talks in the OECD, the IMF, the EEC, and half a dozen other international agencies are going on continuously. There is much talk about accommodating, adjusting, and informing one another, but the fact is that, while there is a lot of talk, countries have not been able to harmonize their policies. Therefore I think it is premature to establish an agency which pools reserves and creates international money- or at least premature to think that such a plan, under present conditions, can work. If we pool reserves and create international money, we are coming very close to setting up an international central bank. I think we should look at the matter in that way, as it immediately raises the question: Are we really ready for such a thing?

Chairman THORP: On the matter of adjustment measures outside the exchange-rate field, a number of members of the conference have asked to speak on the issue of whether emphasis should be placed on the current account or on the capital account. The first is Professor Bloomfield.

BLOOMFIELD: I am not sure on grounds of economic welfare that one can be considered less undesirable than the other, but it may be that one of the reasons for the tendency to choose controls on capital account rather than controls on current account is that the International Monetary Fund authorizes capital controls, whereas the application of controls on current transactions is subject to various international agreements and restraints. It may be that in this country we have chosen capital controls, among other reasons, because they do not involve a violation of the IMF Articles of Agreement.

On the question of whether controls should be market-oriented or administrative, I think that, from the viewpoint of efficiency, we would all favor market-oriented controls. The trouble with the market-oriented controls that we have had is that, in large measure, they have been discriminatory. Take the interest-equalization tax. We have applied it only to certain kinds of capital assets and not to all kinds. And we have applied it only to certain countries rather than to all countries. If we do use market-oriented controls, we ought to try to make them nondiscriminatory.

I would like to raise a question which I hope Eddie Bernstein will answer. When we put the clause in the Bretton Woods agreement about controls over capital movements, what kinds of controls were anticipated, and why—in contrast to our position on current-account controls—did we not put a time limit on them?

Chairman THORP: Can you answer that in sixty seconds, Eddie?

BERNSTEIN: Yes, I can. The first point is that the right to impose capital controls was insistently demanded not only by the Europeans but also by the Americans, who were afraid of prolonged trade discrimination in view of the European payments problem and who wanted such discrimination removed as soon as possible. The second point I would like to make is this: Controls over current-account transactions can also be employed in specific cases where Fund approval has been obtained after consultation. You can have controls over current transactions, but you have to have consultation and approval. And you will not get Fund approval, by the way, for discriminatory controls.

COOPER: I want to make several comments on what has been said earlier today. Although it perhaps reflects the bias of economists to focus on private transactions, the first measures taken to improve the U.S. balance of payments were in the government sector, and they were not on capital account but on trade account. I am referring to the increasingly tight tying of foreign aid to U.S. exports and the adoption of what amounted to a tariff differential of 50 percent or more on government procurement for national defense. Not only were these measures chronologically first but, in my judgment, they are probably the most inefficient of all the devices, restraints, and controls that are now in force. Given the fact that government is here to stay, it is important that we not overlook adjustment measures in the government sector, and I urge that we apply to government transactions any injunctions we apply to private transactions.

My second point is that the shift in emphasis toward capital controls has been due not so much to a preference for capital controls over trade controls on narrow economic-efficiency grounds, as to the assumption that capital restraints are more acceptable to the international community—such measures as the interest-equalization tax and later the voluntary, then mandatory, controls on capital outflow would lead to less retaliation than would restraints on trade. That is to say, the evolution that we have seen has been dominated, not by judgments of economic efficiency, but by considerations of political acceptability and the fear of retaliation.

This conclusion leads me to the point made by Randall Hinshaw and Gottfried Haberler that the United States always has an alternative to the imposition of restraints on capital movement or on trade—namely, to declare the dollar inconvertible into gold. This is certainly true in a technical sense, and from many points of view that alternative has undeniable attractions. It can be argued that the world would not be very much changed in any basic sense if that were done. But the psychological jolt would be extremely acute. This action would play the U.S. trump card, as it were; it would aggressively assert that the world really is on a dollar standard and not on a gold standard—and the action would be interpreted, especially by many continental Europeans, as an act of economic warfare. I am not as sanguine as Professor Haberler that the rest of the world would simply sit back and not respond in any way. I cannot be confident—no one can be confident—about what would happen. But we would run the risk that European governments would take retaliatory action, not in their own economic interests as defined by economists, but for political reasons under nationalistic political pressures. This political consideration has to be taken into account, in my judgment, in considering any particular policy recommendation.

I am sorry that my colleague, Henry Wallich, is not here this morning, because I know that, in contrast to the views expressed here thus far, he much prefers restraints on trade to restraints on capital movement. Trade restrictions offer less disruption to his conception of what the world should ultimately look like, which is one large monetary area. He dislikes capital controls on the ground that they attempt to keep national monetary areas separate from one another. I will not try to argue Henry's case for him, but his point of view does suggest the very broad conclusion that our conceptions of "bliss," as it were, apparently differ greatly around this table. To some of us, bliss represents a world with a single international money—a single monetary union—with fixed exchange rates and with freedom of international transactions, whereas bliss for others apparently also includes freedom of capital transactions, but rationed as between currency areas by movements in exchange rates.

In my view, there is an important difference between these two views of the ideal world—a difference hinging on the degree of factor mobility, and particularly of labor mobility, among the regions of the world. A world of one currency and of fixed exchange rates, but lacking labor mobility, may well lead to what in such a world would be regarded as regional unemployment—perhaps very high regional unemployment. A world of monetary areas, however, or of what Bob Mundell calls optimal currency areas, might be able to handle that regional unemployment problem much more easily. The difference between the two views of the world may also reflect a difference in the political conception of what the world should look like—whether, on the one hand, we should accept nations as they are or, on the other hand, should move toward one world. These differences in world view inevitably influence our individual conceptions of what the adjustment process should look like.

HEILPERIN: I would like to begin by commenting on what has been said thus far in an immensely interesting and, I think, somewhat disturbing discussion.

You may have noticed my unusual silence in the debate over the numerous varieties of fluctuating exchange rates. I don't want any of them. Like Henry Wallich and his dog, the more I hear about flexible rates, the more I prefer fixed parities. I am still an unconverted, and perhaps inconvertible, adherent of fixed parities after all that was said yesterday, and I strongly feel that our objective should be fixed parities without controls. Fixed parities offer an approximation to a single currency, and the absence of controls offers an approximation to a single worldwide economy.

I would have thought that the adjustment process under fixed parities would involve adjustments in trade and capital movements, including movements of short-term funds induced by differential interest rates. I have heard very little to that effect thus far, and I am somewhat frightened, to tell the truth, about the alternatives that Mr. Bergsten has offered to us. We have been offered the choice between controls on trade and controls on capital. The term "market-oriented controls" seems to me a misnomer in this context, because such controls involve an interference with the market system, and I should think that, at the outset of a new Administration, semantics are of some importance.

Gottfried Haberler has told us that he would rather have capital controls than trade controls. Well, if one has to be killed either way, I would agree that perhaps Haberler has chosen the easier way to be killed. But in either case, one would be killed as far as world economics is concerned. Frankly, I have more sympathy with Randall Hinshaw's point of view on trade controls than with Gardner Patterson's. When I reflect that during the 1950's the United States was the great champion of currency convertibility and freer trade, and when I think now of what ten years of entirely needless payments deficits have done to our thinking, I am utterly frightened.

You may be surprised that I don't disagree at all with what Howard Ellis had to say about the gold standard. I have never considered, and I don't consider now, the gold standard as the final point of evolution in monetary affairs. But I think that the establishment of a world currency and of its corollary, a world central bank, will take time. It may take quite a lot of time, because we cannot have a world central bank without many other world institutions, and we are getting more and more deeply involved in nationalism. We are moving backward, not forward. So I would regard the gold standard as a transitional device until we are ready for the Triffin Plan, as expanded and improved by him and others.

Finally, a word about the solution that Gottfried Haberler has mentioned. Certainly, the United States can impose an embargo on gold payments. But I would not take that very lightly. We have seen what happened in 1931 when the United Kingdom imposed an embargo on gold payments. It resulted in a great many complications in the international monetary crisis. And it does no good to speak of Europeans as if they were an undesirable variety of mankind, just because they happen now to have surpluses. For a long time, they had deficits and we had the surpluses. I think we have to work together. In the past, we have workd together through NATO [North Atlantic Treaty Organization], through the Marshall Plan, and later through the OECD. Surely, we don't want to throw all that away just because we have a payments deficit that we are not willing to control. We need a solution that embraces both Europe and ourselves, as well as many other countries. I think, therefore, that an embargo on gold payments would be a very desperate thing to do. I don't agree with those who say that it wouldn't hurt us. It would hurt us very badly.

SOLOMON: Commenting first on what Mr. Heilperin has just said, it seems to me that instead of saying that earlier the United States had surpluses and now is in deficit, what one should say is that earlier the United States had good deficits and now it has bad deficits. It has had deficits almost without interruption since shortly after the end of the war. In the 1930's, of course, the United States had over-all surpluses, for reasons which were largely noneconomic—and perhaps uneconomic as well.

Now a word or two about the questions that were precipitated by Fred Bergsten. Through a powerful effort of will, I will resist the temptation to answer Bob Mundell's comments about Washington policy-makers, except to say that, on the matter of capital controls, it may be useful to remind ourselves that we don't have a very good theory about the efficiency effects of restraints on capital movement. I put this out as a challenge, if I may, Mr. Chairman. I would like to see more work in the literature on this subject. We all know the simple, obvious case for freedom of transactions generally, and I am not quarreling with that in broad terms. But I am not aware of systematic, detailed studies of the welfare or efficiency effects of interference with capital movement, whether the interference is in the form of market-oriented or of administrative controls. I think it would be useful, perhaps essential, to have such studies before we can make the policy judgments that we all seem to be making.

A point that occurs to me in this connection is that, when one makes a case for complete freedom of capital movement, one is probably assuming a set of nation states endowed with fairly similar institutions, capital markets, banking systems, and monetary policies; there are all sorts of assumptions one may have to make before one is sure about the efficiency effects of unfettered capital flow. One does not have to agree completely with Kindleberger and Despres and Walter Salant (they don't fully agree with each other, I think Walter would admit) to recognize that there are institutional differences in capital markets—for example, between the United States and Europe—which may have had something to do with what looked like an excessive tendency for capital to move from the United States and which therefore had something to do with the efforts in Washington to restrict capital outflow. What I am saying does not answer Fred's questions, but it bears on those questions.

Chairman THORP: We have had, you remember, a suggestion that we ought to have a capital outflow from the United States of 1 percent of GNP and another suggestion that the figure should be 10 percent of GNP. Excuse me, Bob.

SOLOMON: I'm delighted to be interrupted by the Chairman. Let me make another point that I haven't heard yet. I think that there has been at least one benefit from the restrictions the United States has imposed on capital flows. We have seen the development in recent years of an enormous international capital market in Europe—the Eurodollar and the Eurobond market. The development of the Eurobond market certainly owes itself in part to the restraints on capital outflow from the United States. American corporations are still buying up Europe with European money, but with long-term European money rather than with liquid dollar balances. Somehow this seems to be a more acceptable system, and it shows up in the balance of payments more favorably, for what that's worth. My main point, however, is that there is a capital market developing in Europe, and I think we need to assess the benefit, if there is a benefit, from this development.

I am fully aware that the remarks I have made will mark me as a controller, which I don't regard myself as; I am afraid of the disfavor of Randall Hinshaw as I speak this way. But with all due respect to Randall, for whom I have great respect, it seems that we should make our judgments on all the issues we're wrestling with, not on theological grounds, but on benefit-cost grounds.

BOURNEUF: In view of the recognized infallibility of E. M. Bernstein on the history of the Fund, I hesitate to suggest that he may have left out one idea when he explained the

Fund position on capital controls. If I recall correctly, in the thinking both on the original Keynes Plan and on the Fund Plan, there was recognition of the problem of using the resources of the Clearing Union or of the Fund to meet capital outflow. At Bretton Woods there was certainly a strong feeling that such massive and erratic capital movements as might occur in the absence of controls would simply make the Fund's resources not big enough. It would seem that the mere size of these movements and their erratic character is what—at least for some of us—makes our attitude toward capital control different from our attitude toward trade control.

BERNSTEIN: It is true that the IMF statutes actually go very strongly along the line that Alice Bourneuf has indicated. Roughly paraphrasing, they say the following: The Fund can *require* as a condition for using its resources that a country with a deficit impose capital controls. This undoubtedly was a big element in the thinking at Bretton Woods.

SILK: This issue of which you like better, trade controls or capital controls, is like being asked whether you want one or two eggs in your beer if you happen to be allergic to eggs.

For an economist, the easiest thing in the world ought to be to oppose trade controls. The efficiency case against trade restrictions is clear, and has been since the days of Adam Smith. One may make short-term exceptions for particular reasons, but I feel from my own experience that those exceptions should be very rare. There is certainly no need, ever, for economists to encourage the business community to get some trade protection. Protection is hard to take away, and it is difficult to prevent escalation of trade controls, once a country starts down that route. So, except in highly unusual circumstances, it is difficult to see any good case to be made for dealing with adjustment problems via trade controls.

Professor Patterson has mentioned one possible exception, which has more to do with trade liberalization than with trade restriction. If you can get differential rates of trade liberalization which will help you to deal with balance-of-payments disequilibria, there is no reason not to do that. In the case of the United States, specifically, we have suffered for a long time from foreign barriers to our exports—for example, European restrictions on our farm products. It is always difficult to add up the score on trade discrimination, but my prejudiced view is that the United States, on balance, is more a victim than a culprit in the world, and before I would accept what Paul Samuelson said about the dollar being overvalued, I would want to know the degree to which U.S. exports are still restricted from foreign markets. So I would be all for differential trade liberalization, including liberalization directed toward our own exports.

On the capital side, I agree with Professor Haberler that, although not a very popular act, capital restriction is preferable to trade restriction. Part of the case for capital controls arises from the problem of massive shifts of funds from one country to another in periods of crisis or threatened crisis. I've talked with Robert Triffin about this, away from the table, and we agree that one of the most destabilizing elements in the world today is the growth of the large multinational corporation which holds many millions of dollars worth of foreign exchange that can be readily moved—and moved, not for speculative reasons, but simply to protect the assets of the corporation. These capital movements do not serve any basic economic purpose; they don't contribute to world economic efficiency or to long-term investment. They are highly disturbing, and may provide a good case for some form of control.

I would agree with Bob Solomon's point that we do not know enough about the efficiency effects of international capital movements. It is not clear to me that interfering with capital movements involves a reduction in economic efficiency every time you interfere; sometimes you might produce the opposite effect. I'm thinking now of specific examples like the Ford company, which moved a lot of dollars into Europe to acquire 100 percent of the assets of British Ford. I find it hard to believe that this transaction, which brought much misery to the Ford company, contributed to world economic efficiency, and I suspect the reverse.

My final point is that in a nationalistic world one might as well be realistic and not plead economic competence, on the one hand, and total ignorance of political factors, on the other. Here again I'm thinking quite specifically of a conversation I had a few years ago with one of our best ambassadors in Europe, who at the time was greatly disturbed about the rise of sentiment in Europe against American takeovers of European business. In my role as a visiting editor, he asked me, "What can we do? Isn't there some way of slowing this down? Isn't it possible to warn American corporations that this trend may not be an entirely good thing?" I responded that perhaps in due time there would be political effects that would retard these acts by American business. Well, those effects have been forthcoming; they haven't been overly disturbing yet, but in other circumstances, they may be extremely so. I think our objectives in this matter can well be called political as well as economic, and we shouldn't be too naive about the objectives of policy from where governments sit.

GARDNER: After listening carefully to the discussion of yesterday and today, I can't help being reminded of the old lady who was treated to a popular explanation of the Einstein theory of relativity. At the end of the lecture, she said, "Well, I'm still confused, but at a higher level."

From the point of view of policy making, it seems very difficult to make hard-and-fast choices among the various alternatives. All we can do is to have some priorities. My own priorities in dealing with the adjustment problem would be along the following lines.

My first priority would be more liquidity, because I entirely agree with Walter Salant and Sir Roy Harrod that, unless we have adequate liquidity, the adjustment problem will be very hard to deal with. We must activate the Special Drawing Rights in adequate amounts. In view of the failure of reserves to grow in the last few years, I would think that something like $5 billion for the first year is the kind of figure we're going to need.

That may not be negotiable. So then we are thrown back to our next priorities. My second priority is to work harder for more effective harmonization of national economic policy, and I want to come back to that theme in a moment, because I have some suggestions to make. My third priority would be to explore the possibility of amending Article XII of the GATT [General Agreement on Tariffs and Trade] in order to have a more effective means of assisting adjustment through the trade mechanism. But I would put the emphasis on differential rates of *reduction* of trade barriers rather than on differential rates of reimposition of barriers—in other words, on getting the surplus countries to accelerate their Kennedy Round cuts or to reduce their border taxes, rather than on seeking adjustment the other way around by increasing restrictions.

On exchange rates, I am frank to say that I don't know enough to make a judgment in this very difficult technical field. Clearly, if we can't do 1, 2, and 3 in this list of priorities, we must at least explore greater flexibility of exchange rates, although—and I say this with some apology, because I can't compete in this highly technical analysis with many of the members here—my own view is that, without accommodating adjustments in the domestic economy, we are not going to get more than some temporary help on the exchange-rate side.

Now let me return to the matter of harmonization of national economic policy, a theme which has been a little neglected in our discussion. It has been said around this table that international institutions must reflect realities, but I would argue that international institutions, such as the IMF and the GATT, can also shape those realities. We have not yet exhausted the possibilities of using international institutions to promote the kind of integrated world we seek.

Unfortunately, the United States has been remarkable in initiating international institutions and then neglecting them, or bypassing them, or using them only in the most narrow and selfish way. We suddenly rush over to GATT to complain about somebody else's restrictions, but then we bypass GATT and bilaterally negotiate quotas for steel and textiles.

We can't have it both ways. If we want to build stronger international institutions to help us, we also have to submit to them on some of the hard cases. Let me be very specific. We pioneered in the United States in the creation of the Fund, then diminished its prestige and effectiveness by moving into the Group of Ten. We talked about strengthening the Fund as an influence on national economic policy, but when it came to our own case, we didn't want to borrow beyond the gold tranche, because we didn't want the Fund telling us what to do. In the case of the GATT, we refused to ratify the International Trade Organization; we refused to accept the Organization for Trade Cooperation, which was our own idea; and we never accepted GATT definitively, so that we still have that pretext for prior inconsistent national legislation. We have never even had legislative authority for our annual financial contribution to the GATT Secretariat. When

I was in the State Department, we used to have to smuggle this through Congress every year under something called "International Conferences and Contingencies." Some contingency! And, except for Gardner Patterson, we have never had an American at the highest level of the GATT Secretariat.

So, when we throw up our hands and say we can't do much through harmonization, I would say that we haven't really tried. If I had time, I could spell out how we haven't even used the OECD, which was our own idea in large part, as fully as we might. To complete my thought, I would say that much more can be done in international institution building to coordinate national economic policies. It is obviously not easy to be optimistic; this is not an effort for one month or one year or ten years, but, as a great American said in another context, "Let us begin!"

BERGSTEN: Just two brief comments, Mr. Chairman. First, I would like to generalize a bit on what Bob Solomon said in answer to my earlier question. He pointed out quite rightly that we really do not have any kind of general theory on the efficiency, plus or minus, of capital controls. It is quite proper to challenge the economics profession in that respect and to throw the matter back to Bob Mundell, so to speak. But I would go beyond that and say that whereas we do have theoretical work on the gains from trade, dating from Adam Smith through Paul Samuelson, we have only recently begun to get some analysis, primarily through Harry Johnson, of the costs of protection. That work is by no means complete, and it is by no means clear as a policy guide. And we have as yet no general theory, such as we do have on the trade side, of the gains from freedom of capital movement. Until we have something like that, it is very difficult to make a judgment on whether it is better to have free capital movement, with some restricting of trade, or vice versa. I think it is unfair for anyone to say that the scientific community has provided us with all the answers and that all that people in government have to do is to apply those answers.

On another theoretical matter, Walter Salant made the immensely interesting and important point that, under a fixed exchange-rate system, the pressures that result are for surplus countries to inflate and for deficit countries to deflate, whereas under a flexible-rate system the pressures would be for deficit countries to inflate and for surplus countries to deflate. I have put this in an oversimplified way, but that would appear to be the general conclusion. It is fascinating to look at this conclusion in the context of dilemma cases, which I think we agreed are the really difficult cases under a fixed-rate system. In a fixed-rate model, the dilemma cases are where the surplus country has full employment and where the deficit country has underemployment. And the exact results that Walter Salant pointed out would result from flexible rates are those which we would want to see in the dilemma cases I have just described.

To be specific, the surplus country with full employment ought to be in a position where there is downward pressure on its price level rather than the upward pressure that occurs under fixed exchange rates; conversely, the deficit country with underemployment ought to have pressure on it which would be in an expansionary direction. In both cases, the desired result would occur through greater exchange-rate flexibility. In the nondilemma cases under a fixed-rate system, the introduction of a flexible rate might in some cases operate in the wrong direction, and one might have to trade off the losses on that side for the gains on the other. But it is quite clear that the pressures which would result under flexible exchange rates would be in the right direction from an adjustment standpoint in the dilemma cases that now plague us under a fixed-rate system.

EXTER: I first want to amend a statement made by Howard Ellis. He had the impression that I think we are going to have a crash. I didn't say that, although I may have said something to make him think that I was apprehensive about the future! It was my good friend, Randolph Burgess, who said yesterday that the present situation bears an unmistakable resemblance to 1929. Suffice it to say that the credit pyramid we have built in the 1960's is much larger than the credit pyramid we built in the 1920's.

Yesterday, I gave you my version of the franc-mark crisis of November 1968. Today, we have exactly the same elements of a crisis that we had in November, and I should not be at all surprised if we soon see a repetition of a good deal of what happened then. Having phoned New York this morning, I can tell you that the pound sterling has been erratic today; the French franc is weak and is being supported by the Bank of France and the Federal Reserve Bank of New York; the mark is strong; the Swiss franc is strong; and the price of gold has gone up. In my view, the fact that the French did not have exchange controls last November and do have harsh controls now makes no difference whatsoever. I share Randall Hinshaw's "religious" abhorrence of trade and exchange controls; they turn moral forces upside down, penalizing the honest man and rewarding the rascal. And there will be plenty of rascals to convert French francs, and other currencies as well, into marks again. If controls prevent equilibrium forces from working through the honest, they work through the dishonest.

In closing, I see two essential differences between my views and those of many others around the table. First, my model of the way the world works—the international adjustment process—is different. Second, I regard gold as the basic money. I don't think we can demonetize it. On the contrary, it is paper money that is being demonetized.

We seem to have learned so little from the past. I would like to read what Charles Mackay said in 1852 in the preface to his *Memoirs of Extraordinary Popular Delusions and the Madness of Crowds*: "Money has often been a cause of the delusion of multitudes. Sober nations have all at once become desperate gamblers and risked almost their existence upon the turn of a piece of paper. . . . Men, it has been well said, think in herds; it will be seen that they go mad in herds, while they only recover their senses slowly, and one by one."

Chairman THORP: The next member of the herd to speak is Professor Douglass.

GORDON K. DOUGLASS: I would like to return for a moment to "Bergsten's Choice."

The evidence is growing that the volume of international trade which can be accounted for by differential rates of innovation and imitation among nations is increasing rapidly—so rapidly, indeed, that a fairly significant share of trade is now in new, research-intensive goods. Temporary monopolies, it seems, in addition to narrow price and cost comparisons à la Heckscher-Ohlin, are emerging as a primary basis for trade.

Under these conditions, international adjustment through greater exchange-rate flexibility is less likely to work well than in a trading world of unadulterated differences of relative factor endowments. Thus we may need to couple more flexible exchange rates with some kinds of direct or indirect control.

Imitation is made possible by international communication, usually through the medium of direct investment, international licensing arrangements, or competitive research and development. Before we can choose wisely between restrictions on trade and restrictions on capital movement, as Mr. Bergsten has asked us to do, we must ask what impact any given menu of controls might have on various methods of communicating new ideas to the "catching-up" countries. I, for one, would want to explore the growth effects as well as the efficiency effects of capital controls—especially controls on direct investment—before endorsing the capital controls approach.

BURGESS: I sympathize a great deal with Michael Heilperin and John Exter regarding the nature of our present problem. How did we get that way? It seems to me that over a period of years we've been busy at home and abroad in gradually removing, one after another, the more automatic pressures for adjustment. Certainly, we have done this at home with the Federal Reserve System, and other countries have been moving in the same direction.

Now we are not going back and reimpose a whole series of automatic adjustment devices. Dr. Ellis was quite right in reviewing that position. But I was tremendously interested that he came to the point of saying that there should be somebody who can say "no." That is where the present machinery is inadequate. Dick Gardner has made a very important point—that we need to start with the institutions we have and gradually build them to greater strength. The IMF does have the authority, as Eddie Bernstein has pointed out, to say "no" in more ways than the public realizes, but it does not have the support and pressure of public opinion for going far enough in the direction of being an international central bank. What I'm saying, in effect, is what Henry Wallich said earlier—that under any system we must have discipline. And we haven't got it. We are not going to get it by re-establishing an automatic gold standard or any other automatic mechanism, but we must recognize that the lack of discipline is there, and must try to restore it through the institutions we build.

HARROD: I would like to make two or three special points,

and will begin with foreign feelings about the United States. I did detect an omission. One of our members referred to feelings which militated against the establishment of the dollar as a world currency—in particular, the feeling against American capital searching out business opportunities in Europe. That feeling doesn't exist, I think, in the United Kingdom, but it is undoubtedly a fact in certain quarters in Europe.

But there is another more general point about the dollar as a world currency. Though I've heard the point made in American conferences, I don't think I've heard it mentioned this weekend. I shall remind you of it, as it is a more subtle matter than mere nationalism.

Suppose we think of the dollar as the world currency. In that case, we want an annual increment of, say, $3 billion—to name a moderate figure—for which the United States has to have an over-all deficit of $3 billion. Now does it make sense for the various nations of the world, widely spread, to pay in real resources $3 billion a year in exchange for bits of paper? For we are talking about a transfer of real resources every year—a transfer of real resources to the richest country in the world. To put the matter another way, the United States issues the currency and takes a 100 percent seignorage charge on it; I've heard that statement at a conference in this country.

You may say, "Well, it's very nice that the United States is providing the world with money." But couldn't there be some other way of supplying the world with money in sufficient quantity? One possibility would be through something like the Stamp Plan, which I suppose is dead; in that case, it would be the less developed countries that would get the $3 billion a year in real resources. But they're poor people; it might make sense for them to receive the $3 billion annual seignorage charge—that is, to get something for nothing—but it hardly makes sense for the recipient to be the richest country in the world. And I would add that it isn't quite fair to call this an anti-American point or an expression of nationalist sentiment.

On another matter, we have heard much around this table about control of capital movement. The underlying assumption seems to be that if you reduce the outflow of capital, you are helping the balance of payments. But is that true? It all depends on your time horizon. There is nothing sacred about a year. If you have a sufficient time horizon—and it doesn't have to be a very long one—you are hurting the balance of payments when you reduce the outflow of capital.

Take the case of the United States. Suppose that the restraint of capital outflow had started around the end of 1957, when the U.S. deficit rose sharply and, as Mr. Solomon said, changed from a good deficit to a bad deficit. Suppose the interest-equalization tax and the other capital restraints had been in effect throughout the past eleven years. Would the U.S. balance of payments have been better or worse? I suggest that it would have been worse.

BERNSTEIN: It would have been just the same.

HARROD: Why the same?

BERNSTEIN: Because we would have had the same direct investment financed through the issue of corporate bonds instead of through the issue of Treasury notes to monetary authorities.

HARROD: Well, sir, you're being too particular; I'm making the general point. I'm talking about the restraint on capital outflow as a matter of general principle. People assume that it is good for the balance of payments. It may be so if you have a year's horizon. But if you have an eleven-year horizon, it hurts the balance of payments, because the interest, the profit, and the repayments will soon exceed the annual rate of capital investment. You can see this very clearly from the U.S. balance-of-payments figures.

And I would say that you have the same problem in reverse with the less developed countries. They ought to think very carefully about allowing too much capital inflow. India knows that perfectly well. The problem is that the inflow of capital must grow at a sort of snowballing rate—at an impracticable rate—to prevent the service charges from exceeding that inflow. As in our other case, this problem is concealed if our time horizon is only a year.

My third point is that I hope some of you will study the British devaluation, which is extremely interesting so far, though the whole scene may change. Devaluation seems to have had an almost startlingly good effect on British exports. In volume, they've gone up 16 percent. That's quite a big jump. At the same time, there are some curious features about this devaluation. One is that the average prices of

British exports, in sterling, have gone up about 10 percent. People talk about an export-led expansion in the United Kingdom, which is a true description in a way, but one might also call it an export-led inflation, because the rise in export prices is by far the biggest inflationary factor in Britain since devaluation.

I don't have up-to-the-minute figures, but the rise in the cost of living has been of the order of 5 percent, and the rise in wage rates of the order of 6 percent, so that real wages have increased by about 1 percent. As productivity has certainly increased by more than 1 percent, real wages have risen less than productivity. At the same time, the economy has been very sluggish. Consumption has only gone up by 2 percent in 1968, over what was a low level in 1967. Yet all of this has been accompanied by a colossal increase in imports of manufactured goods—an increase which has almost offset the increase in British exports. In other categories, such as food and raw materials, imports have gone up at a more or less regular rate; there have been certain variations in stockpiling, but there has been nothing extraordinary about 1968. What has been extraordinary is that, in spite of devaluation, there has been this abnormally strong rise in imports of manufactured goods.

Contrary to majority opinion, I think that the trouble on the import side results from the stagnant state in which the economy is kept by persistent deflationary policies. The home market is growing so slowly that it is hardly worth cultivating. On exports, British manufacturers have gone all out. That's excellent, but at the same time the economy is distinctly underemployed. You may ask, Why the big expansion of imports? Because, from a foreign standpoint, the whole thing is different. For foreign manufacturers, it may be worthwhile to engage in tremendous selling campaigns in the United Kingdom, because only for them is it a big fresh market available for capture. I think the relation is not symmetrical here; it isn't worthwhile for the British to make great efforts to sell more in their home market—and they are not encouraged to—while for foreigners the United Kingdom is a big new market, where they may be in a position to make big gains.

I am not solving the problem; I'm merely leaving you with this pattern to think about. I am suggesting that the problem is not so simple as to be solved merely by devaluing the currency or introducing a flexible exchange rate. It is a more complicated matter, and I would ask you to give it thought.

Chairman THORP: Thank you very much. I think Bob Triffin wants to give it some immediate thought.

TRIFFIN: My remarks are concerned with the earlier part of Sir Roy's statement.

It seems rather paradoxical that one of the major objections to my own proposal has always been that it allegedly involves impossible surrender of sovereignty. I find this strange, because, if we are to run an international monetary system, it must be run somehow; somebody must decide how much reserves are going to be created, and somebody must decide how they are to be used. As several members of the conference have reminded us, we are now essentially and broadly on a dollar system. This means that those decisions are made by us Americans, and it also means that the world monetary system is run as a by-product of American domestic monetary policy. This does not involve much surrender of sovereignty for *us* as long as the system lasts, but it certainly involves total surrender of sovereignty by every other nation in the world.

The alternative to the present system either is some sort of international monetary system, under international management, or it is chaos. I think that the surrender of sovereignty that would be involved for the United States in accepting an international monetary system is much less than people think, because in practice, no matter what the formal system is, the United States would remain a very big country with a very big influence on international decisions. Even if we made big mistakes and had large deficits, other countries would be very worried about the impact of forcing us to redress the situation overnight through deflation, devaluation, or other methods.

To link this with what Sir Roy was saying, I think it is undoubtedly true that the world will require the creation of several billions of dollars of credit reserves every year, and that the only solution which in the long run will be acceptable is one in which every country has some sort of voice. Sir Roy has suggested that what is needed is something like the Stamp Plan, in which the new reserves would first accrue to the less developed countries. I think that promoting economic development is a useful purpose in reserve creation, but it is not the only one. There are all kinds of other international purposes on which everybody agrees. Everybody agrees with stabilization loans by the IMF; the Fund has been engaged in such operations for the last twenty years. That, of course, involves surrender of sovereignty in the sense that, if a country does not agree with the IMF about its stabilization program, it will not get the money. But the country is sovereignly free to reject the advice of the IMF and to go its own way without the IMF policy and without the IMF financing.

I would like to say another word about linking reserve creation with economic development. As you know, the Group of Ten felt that this should be absolutely taboo; one must not finance long-term investment with short-term liabilities. I will not go into the economics of that, but I would like to make two points. In the first place, this is actually the situation which prevailed when the sterling standard was running successfully in the nineteenth century, and the same statement can be made about the dollar standard in the early 1950's. These two reserve-center countries were borrowing short from the countries that accumulated sterling or dollar balances as reserves, and were relending long—in large part, to underdeveloped countries. In the second place, it seems curious to me that those gentlemen who thought that we must not make long-term investments with short-term money decided nearly overnight to use short-term money to make *gifts*, since 70 percent of the Special Drawing Rights that are used are not subject to reconstitution. That is to say, more than two-thirds of a country's SDR's can clearly be regarded as an outright gift, with no strings attached. And the chief beneficiary, of course, will be the United States. I think that in the long run it is inconceivable that the rest of the world, without having any voice in our policies, will agree to use this new facility for the primary purpose of making gifts to the richest country in the world.

ALLEN: My first point is that economists have much to be modest about, which gives me pause in advocating the extension of powers of discretionary policy-making. My second point is that economists have much to be sad about if, in fact, there must be an expansion of such policy-making powers. Let me try to illustrate these two points with a version of some of the things that have been said around this table, but let me assure you that the points do not depend on entirely adequate representations of statements by any person here. I offer this disclaimer, for I fear that I may, in fact, misquote.

In connection with my first point, I seem to have been told a number of unexpected things in the last three days. Let me list some of them. I have heard, for example, that with respect to a situation of excess demand, otherwise labeled inflation, imports are not a function either of exchange rates or of the money stock. On a second matter, I think I have heard that we have nonpositively sloped supply curves, demand curves which are perfectly vertical, and marginal propensities to import which are equal to unity. I also have the impression from some of the things that have been said that exchange rates are not real prices which really equilibrate real markets.

Countries have a high propensity to peg rates, I am told, and they are rational in thus seeking stability in an uncertain world—as though the performance of a market is to be properly judged by the degree of price stability it displays. Next, the international monetary or adjustment system, I am told, has worked well since 1946 or 1949 or 1960, except for the last two or three or five years. Note that the span from 1960 to 1964 is not a very long Golden Age and that the system worked well *except* for the United States and the United Kingdom and some others along the way.

Indeed, I am told that, even now, the *system* is fine; it is only *countries* which have difficulties. Thus, on the one hand, I am told that the system is basically attractive, adjustment does work, and the prosperity of the prosperous part of the world can be imputed to the system. On the other hand, I am told that there are serious inadequacies in the system and crises in its operation. Significant changes and developments continue, and further surgery or at least loving care is in order, with each consultant possessing his own scheme of reform, typically concerned more with liquidity than with adjustment. Finally, there have been numerous disconcerting references to the subject of freely fluctuating exchange rates, and doubt has even been expressed that the matter could be taken seriously by expert opinion.

For example, flexible rates, I am told, are unacceptable, but fixed rates make no contribution to adjustment. I am told, with fixed rates, internal adjustments are in order, but that wage rates have not maintained relations with productivity which are appropriate for adjustment. A crawling peg, I am told, would not necessarily destroy expectations of a large rate change, and is relevant only to real or structural changes, which typically are gradual. I am told that, while it is unacceptable to leave rates free to vary widely and wildly, management of rates to iron out undue fluctuations is very difficult and risky in several respects. There is a tendency for management to peg, pegging is generally at an overvaluation level, it is difficult to move a pegged rate, and there is a strong tendency to introduce restrictions. Finally, most disconcerting of all, I am told that government advisers are not infinitely wise.

Now my second point, which is briefer. In my opening statement of two days ago, I contended that there simply is no adjustment mechanism under the IMF agreement. I was initially under the impression that Frank Southard intended to rebut this contention when he noted several country cases of effective adjustment, but it seemed to me that the supposed rebuttal missed the mark. Lack of a mechanism, after all, is consistent in various happy cases with a resolution of balance-of-payments problems, and existence of happy cases is not tantamount to existence of a mechanism. But it is clear now that Mr. Southard and I were not really talking about the same thing. For while my reference was to a *mechanism* of adjustment, he, along with others, was referring to a *method* of adjustment—a method which might be ad hoc or by formula, using tools which might or might not be conventional, but in any case something other, and I think less, than a mechanism.

It may be that, in this veil of tears and scarcity, contrived method is better than market mechanism. If so, I should take that as a manifestation of the curse of original sin and as evidence that there is no very attractive solution. Second-best would seem the very best we have, and I should think it only decent and genteel that we busy people of affairs occasionally pause in our work of running the world and deeply feel sorrow that more of the burden cannot be borne by the market.

OLIVER: In thinking about the angels of this particular conference, one is obliged to support Randall Hinshaw's position that the world is better off with fewer controls rather than more—particularly those kinds of controls which interfere with efficiency. And I take it there is general agreement with Dick Gardner's position that harmonization, while not easily attainable, is highly desirable, and with Howard Ellis's position that the world would be better off if it had a greater degree of liquidity, so that the problem of adjustment wouldn't have to occur with such frequency.

I must say, though, that I have more and more come to feel that the real angel of the conference is Eddie Bernstein, for he represents people who formulated the Bretton Woods agreement. As I have listened to our discussion, I have marvelled more than I ever did before that agreement was reached at Bretton Woods, that such a good plan as the International Monetary Fund materialized at all. This has led me to the conclusion that perhaps the international organizations we now have may, with some necessary adjustments, succeed in serving us reasonably well in the future.

Beyond this, I would advance the proposition that the most difficult aspect of the adjustment problem is *knowing when a fundamental disequilibrium exists.* I assume from the debate here that almost everybody is in agreement that, if a country *does* have a fundamental disequilibrium, an exchange-rate change of some sort is called for. All our discussion of whether we should have a crawling peg or a wider band or big jumps or prongs has rested on the conclusion that we will correct payments disequilibria through exchange-rate changes. The difficulty is deciding when the disequilibrium is severe enough to call for alterations in exchange rates. But if we cannot agree that the United States or France or Germany is in fundamental disequilibrium today or that Britain was in fundamental disequilibrium four years ago or three years ago, then it is very difficult for us to agree upon precisely what the adjustment mechanism should be.

While there is unanimous, or almost unanimous, agreement that fundamental disequilibrium should be dealt with by exchange-rate changes, some of us are of the view that in less serious situations, payments difficulties should be remedied by what they regard as less severe measures, such as temporary controls on trade or on capital movement. But how long is temporary, and what are the political problems of exchange-rate changes? These crucial questions have not been answered.

My last point concerns optimum currency areas. One of our members has said that, in a sense, the entire world is the optimum currency area. That is true, of course, in a Triffin Plan sort of world, where we have a world central bank managing a world currency. But a world of several, or many, currency areas needs to be considered. I would advance the suggestion that one criterion for an optimum currency area is whether, in a given area, it is possible *institutionally* to harmonize internal policies in such a way that the area is able to maintain a reasonable degree of price-level stability and full employment. But having agreed on what an optimum currency area is, we would still have to agree on how to adjust exchange rates between such areas, and that is the difficult matter.

BERNSTEIN: In one of his many points, Professor Allen may have hit on the real division of opinion here. About two or three months ago, Frank Schiff, the Deputy Undersecretary for Monetary Affairs at the Treasury, telephoned me to ask, "When did they first use the term, 'adjustment process'? Is it something new?" I told him I would do my best to find the answer. Naturally, I did the obvious thing; I pulled out Viner's *Studies in the Theory of International Trade.* Viner has a chapter entitled, "The Mechanism of Adjustment." This is the term that Professor Allen hit on; a mechanism of adjustment is what he wants.

And that is the difference between us. There are some people here who want a mechanism of adjustment, whether it's the gold standard, which is one sort of automatic mechanism, or freely fluctuating exchange rates, which is another mechanism, whereas most of us around this table really want a *process* of adjustment. A process of adjustment would mean, not that the international monetary system must necessarily regenerate stability when that's disturbed, but that individual governments follow policies which restore equilibrium—policies which might, by the way, include any of the various alternatives we have discussed in the direction of greater exchange-rate flexibility.

Personally, I am at neither extreme on this issue. For example, I agree wholeheartedly that it is not desirable to give an international agency great leeway in deciding what it thinks is the best policy for the world. One difficulty, of course, is that we are not all wise. We know that. The other difficulty is that an international policy by an international agency has to be something like an average of what the individual policies would be. Suppose, for example, that the amount of reserves to be created each year by an international agency will vary with its opinion. The surplus countries will say, "We're getting too much reserves; the deficit countries are generating inflation"; and the deficit countries will of course want reserve creation to be as large as possible. The amount of new reserves created under these conditions may make far less sense than a planned steady increase that is not entrusted to the discretion of an international agency.

Professor Allen has referred to my statement that the adjustment mechanism has not really worked badly except in the case of the United States. The United States is, of course, a very important exception, but I don't think I have made clear why it is an exceptional case. The U.S. balance of payments is unique in this important respect: the proportion of payments which are made on a purely political basis—and therefore are not responsive to economic policy—is enormously large. We don't vary our troop expenditures on the ground that the balance of payments is weak, and it is very difficult to cut foreign aid merely because we have a balance-of-payments problem. So the United States does have this very big batch of payments that is not responsive to economic policy. In addition, we have another big batch of payments, the capital outflow, that is not readily responsive to domestic policy—and, where it is responsive, there is an excessive effect on the domestic economy relative to the benefit to the balance of payments.

On top of these unique features, there isn't any doubt in my mind that the coincidence of a war boom and an investment boom has brought a very rapid increase in aggregate demand in the United States. This excessive aggregate demand has manifested itself in two ways—in a rise in domestic prices and in excessive imports. The deterioration in the U.S. balance of payments on current account is the thing that has really hurt. Our current-account surplus has dropped from \$8.5 billion in 1964 to \$2.5 billion in 1968. Sir Roy is right; the world isn't going to keep on giving us goods, services, and capital assets in exchange for dollars, particularly if in the process we are spreading inflation to other areas.

Thus I wouldn't jump to the conclusion that the root of all our difficulties is our adjustment system. The first step in getting a good adjustment process is to get rid of the inflationary pressures in the United States. We want to do that anyway. I venture to say that if we could improve our current-account surplus, if we could stop our rise in prices or slow it down materially, we would find that the European surplus countries would be very prepared to make the adjustments that would go with such a balance of payments in the United States.

I rather agree with Mundell; the United States is unique, and it was unique under the gold standard. Under the gold standard, how was adjustment divided between the surplus countries and the deficit countries? The answer is very simple; it was divided between them in proportion to the size of their monetary economies. This means that if the United States had a surplus and the Philippines had a deficit, 100 percent of the adjustment was made by the Philippines and zero by us. Or if we had the deficit and the Dutch had the surplus, it means that 90 percent of the adjustment was made by the Dutch and 10 percent by us. I submit that, even if we were to retain the gold-exchange standard, the Europeans would not object to making an adjustment which involved, say, the acquisition of $1 billion a year, or even a larger sum. I agree with Sir Roy that they would prefer some other method where we don't get all the real resources even for the income-earning assets that we give them. But, in my opinion, if we succeeded in stabilizing our own domestic economy without deflating, without causing large unemployment—just stopping the inflation—the rest of the world would be prepared to make the adjustments to whatever the balance of payments requires.

I would not threaten anybody. I would not stop studying the various proposals for improving the adjustment system. I am perfectly willing, myself, to consider all sorts of variants in the exchange system as such. Certainly the rest of the world wants prosperity; it doesn't want deflation here. Therefore, if the United States, as the prime mover in the world, were to show the responsibility that a country of its size and importance should show in promoting the stability and prosperity of its own economy, we would find that the adjustment process works reasonably well and that what additional flexibility is needed would be forthcoming.

ALLEN: I appreciate the remarks of Mr. Bernstein and the spirit in which they were given. I will add only this: I too want a process, but a process engendered by, and stemming from, a market mechanism.

ELLSWORTH: I would like to ask Eddie Bernstein a question in connection with what he's just said. Suppose that, in order to maintain our foreign policies for aid, military expenditures, and reasonably free capital movements, we need a surplus on current account of the order of $8 billion a year, as we had back in 1964. Do you really think that the other countries would allow, through up-valuation of the mark or up-valuation of several currencies, this degree of adjustment to take place?

BERNSTEIN: I think, Paul, that on this matter I would make a distinction between the current-account surplus and the trade surplus. I do think that an $8 billion current-account surplus would be acceptable to the world, but I agree that if we need a *trade* surplus of that magnitude, it might mean forcing out the United Kingdom, Germany, and Japan from the market of supplying sophisticated goods for export. They would resist it. I might add that they would resist it just as much with fluctuating rates. They do want a share of the market for exporting sophisticated industrial goods. But with an $8 billion current-account surplus, of which perhaps close to $4 billion would be in services if we brought our military expenditures down to pre-Vietnam levels, the accompanying trade surplus would not be intolerable.

Chairman THORP: Of course, we could divert a good deal of the surplus into the aid program, if we really set ourselves to it, without causing quite the same complications. Mr. Mundell.

MUNDELL: The international monetary system should function in such a way as to assure the stability and growth of the world economy. That objective, as I have repeatedly said, is closely tied to the stability of the U.S. economy. In the past three years, the United States has not been in a conflict position; it has been in a position of inflation and balance-of-payments deficit, and the proper remedy for that situation—I think it has been established for a hundred years or so—is to stop the inflation and correct the deficit through monetary policy.

This is cheap advice, of course, because everyone knows it and they have known it for a long time. It is cheap advice, also, because of the great difficulty of applying the brakes or shifting gears in an economy like the United States, without throwing the economy into reverse. It is not even a simple matter to change the rate of monetary expansion from 7 percent to 4 percent, because jerking the rate of monetary expansion in that way can produce all sorts of flips and jumps. I agree with at least one thing that Bill Allen said—that in this area we do not understand what happens when we work in terms of third derivatives, or changes in rates of change.

But let us suppose that we can get our inflation under control and correct our payments problem. Then we have to recognize that France and Britain are in balance-of-payments weakness and that dealing effectively with U.S. problems is going to cause enormous difficulties for the franc and for the pound sterling.

In this connection, I agree with Sir Roy Harrod that the world is in too tight a position with respect to liquidity. We do need a big dose of liquidity or, to put it more correctly, a big change in the quality of the liquidity that we have. Take the tremendous proliferation of swaps as a means of dealing with this problem. Eddie Bernstein would have the best number on this; the figure may be $10 billion or $12 billion in the last two years. Whatever the figure is, swaps are a very dangerous and unstable sort of liquidity. We need to move very quickly toward some kind of centralization of reserves, whether through Triffin's plan, or Machlup's plan, or mine, or any of the others.

I think we agree more on the fundamentals than we disagree on the details. We should move forward on the fundamentals and stop worrying about the details, because our differences are far smaller than the difference between not doing anything and doing one of the things that we could do.

CHAPTER VI

CONCLUDING OBSERVATIONS

In his role as moderator, Professor Machlup made the closing statement of the conference, ably summarizing the views of the other members and his reactions to those views. Occasionally, his remarks were interrupted by comments from those around the table; these comments are reproduced at the points where they occurred.

R.H.

Chairman THORP: We started this conference with the wisdom of Fritz Machlup, and now we will see if all our discussion has had any impact whatsoever, or whether Fritz merely repeats to us the ideas he expounded at the beginning.

MACHLUP: Mr. Chairman, I am not sufficiently impressed with my ideas to repeat them too often. Of course, what is "too often" is for me to judge.

Let me say, first of all, that if economists are people who, almost by definition, disagree among themselves as well as with outsiders, then this conference of experts is not typical. For, on some major issues, our experts have arrived—or had arrived before they arrived here—at a consensus that closely approaches unanimity. To be sure, we have taken no polls. Thus it may be illegitimate for me to fabricate quantitative evidence for my assertion of consensus. Nevertheless, you may wish to hear my findings, which are based on a careful reading of my notes.

My first finding is that all the participants, without exception, want change of one kind or another in international monetary arrangements in order to facilitate adjustment. While dissatisfaction with the manner in which existing institutions have affected the adjustment process has ranged all the way from mild frowns to severe censure and downright rejection, all the conferees believe that change is desirable or urgently needed to make adjustment easier.

Only two of the thirty-nine participants, Michael Heilperin and John Exter, want this change to take the form of a return to an automatic or semi-automatic gold standard, though we all regret that a third member of this small minority has been unable to join us at this conference. Let me take this occasion to convey our greetings and good wishes to Jacques Rueff, who would have added his voice and eloquence to the standard arguments for the gold standard. The other thirty-seven monetary experts here have remained nonbelievers.

Advocacy of an automatic or semi-automatic gold standard, with gold as the sole reserve medium, is not to be confused with advocacy of an increase in the official price of gold, as one can be in favor of the latter without being in favor of the former. Two, three, or perhaps four in our group would favor a higher official price for gold, though for different reasons. Sir Roy Harrod, I believe, is the only member who wants the price hike in order to saturate the international payments system with liquidity by creating at one stroke $40 billion or more of additional reserves. This is not what the other gold-price boosters want, nor does any other member of this conference.

While on the subject of gold, perhaps I may add that a theological analogy may be quite appropriate. Recently, there have been two schools of thought in theology, and it may be quite proper, with a slight change, to apply the analogy to international monetary thinking. One is the school which pronounces, "Gold is dead," whereas the other school says, "In Gold we trust." I think you will clearly recognize John Exter as belonging to the second school. I refrain from saying that he prays to the Golden Calf, even though he appears to be using the apex of a pyramid as a place of worship.

I come now to another issue on which I have taken a score—the important issue of exchange-rate flexibility. Six members of our group did not express themselves on this subject, so I do not know to which party they belong. Of the other thirty-three, I found five opposed to greater flexibility and twenty-eight in favor. Of the twenty-eight, six merely wanted greater flexibility through more frequent discrete adjustments of the exchange rate, while twenty-two were in favor of a more continuous, gliding adjustment of the parity. If my tally is correct, Eddie Bernstein, Arthur Bloomfield, Alice Bourneuf, Sir Roy Harrod, Bob Mundell, and Frank Southard were those who felt that greater exchange-rate flexibility should be achieved merely by providing inducements for making jumps when needed, rather then delaying them too long.

Two other approaches to greater flexibility, the wider band and the crawling peg, might be used together. It was Bob Solomon, I believe, who asked how we could make countries use the wider band if they are now unwilling to make more frequent jumps. Well, that is exactly the purpose of the system—to reduce the reluctance of making exchange-rate adjustments. As to the gliding parity, there have been serious questions raised of how it should be accomplished—whether the crawls should be by formula, whether they should be by discretion, and whether, in either case, they could be expected to be in the right direction. It is certainly possible that the crawling peg, whether it crawls by formula or by discretion, might crawl in the wrong direction, and more thought is needed on how to guard against such a possibility.

A fourth system of greater flexibility was proposed by Robert Triffin; it might be called the system of limiting the permissible accumulation and depletion of reserves. I question the appropriateness of calling it the "prong" system, because few would know what the prong refers to. What Triffin really wants is this: Instead of determining limits to the fluctuations in exchange rates, he wants to establish limits to the fluctuations in reserves; when reserves have risen or fallen to the limits, the monetary authorities would not be permitted to peg the exchange rate any longer, and the country would have to allow its currency to appreciate or depreciate in the foreign-exchange market. By the way, this system was actually practiced in Canada for over ten years, and Don Marsh, of the Royal Bank of Canada, has been advocating its re-adoption by Canada and other countries.

There are difficulties with this system, as I am sure Triffin recognizes. One problem is how to measure reserves, since we all know how easy it is for a central bank to hide additions to its reserves or to conceal reserve losses through swap arrangements with commercial banks. Albert Hahn has often told us how skillfully the German central bank could hide an increase in its dollar reserves by passing them on to the commercial banks under swap (repurchase) agreements.

With such maneuvers, there is at least a question whether reserves can be measured with any precision at all.

TRIFFIN: That problem was solved in the EPU [European Payments Union].

MACHLUP: Well, I'm glad to hear there are problems that can be solved and *were* solved.

Finally, of course, we have the alternative of a system of freely flexible exchange rates—a system of unlimited and unmanaged flexibility. As I have indicated earlier, this system appears to be a highly extreme ideal type, since its adoption seems to be incompatible with the nature of central bankers. I cannot imagine a central banker, at least among those living today, who would resist his "propensity to peg." It may be a contradiction in terms: a central banker is a man who *has* to intervene.

In discussing flexibility, we need to guard against several widespread confusions. I cannot warn enough against the confusion of "flexible" with "fluctuating." Exchange rates may be flexible without fluctuating. Let me warn also against the confusion between "flexible" and "unstable." Actually, the system of fixed parities has probably led to more unstable exchange rates than might have prevailed under certain systems of rate flexibility. Finally, flexible need not mean "actually variable." The word flexible has to be defined from the point of view of a particular monetary authority or nation. The exchange rate between country A and country B is subject to policies by two monetary authorities. It is quite possible that the exchange rate is flexible from the viewpoint of country A and fixed from the viewpoint of country B. In other words, country A does nothing to keep the exchange rate from moving, yet the rate may not move because country B prevents it from moving.

Thus, several economists who talk about the United States under a flexible-rate regime do not believe that the exchange rate of the dollar would move at all. Flexibility for the United States would simply mean that the United States would not do anything to keep the rate from moving. If country B wished to peg its currency against the dollar, then of course that exchange rate would not move, although it would remain flexible from the point of view of the United States.

This is an important insight, and it answers an objection

made by Henry Wallich, who said that the United States cannot take the initiative and therefore cannot get the intended results of variations in exchange rates. Indeed, the United States *can* take the initiative if it wants to, but it may also achieve much merely by making the exchange rate flexible from its own point of view, leaving any pegging or unpegging to others. If other countries peg their currencies to the dollar by buying all the dollars that are offered to them, there will not be any variation in exchange rates, but in that case the United States will not need any rate variation: it will have the benefit of the voluntary and involuntary capital movements from countries investing in the dollars. This capital movement should not be counted as financing a payments deficit of the United States, even on a liquidity basis, provided there is no conversion into U.S. gold.

On the transition to flexible exchange rates, it was interesting to hear from the two experts on the Fund Articles of Agreement, Eddie Bernstein and Frank Southard, that the Articles impose no serious obstacle to greater flexibility. There is certainly no obstacle to the crawl; the very small changes in parity that would occur under the system of crawling pegs are perfectly compatible with the Fund Articles. The wider band would, of course, offend against the language of the Articles, but experience has shown that the Fund has been willing to tolerate lapses from the 1 percent rule. The Fund overlooked infractions of that rule in the case of multiple exchange rates; it overlooked them in the case of Canada for a period of twelve years; it overlooks them now in the case of Chile and Brazil. So we probably would not find the IMF objecting to greater flexibility of exchange rates, though it might perhaps be wise, sooner or later, to change the language of the Articles of Agreement.

BERNSTEIN: The Fund wouldn't interfere with any transitional use of fluctuating rates, but in good faith, there would need to be a change in the Articles if this were to be a permanent change in policy.

MACHLUP: Yes, in good faith; the question is how formidable this proviso is in practical politics.

Whether the transition to greater flexibility should take place through a multinational agreement is another hard question to answer. I believe such an approach would be difficult; most nations may refuse even to sit down and discuss the matter, for fear of massive speculative capital movements. They may not want to sit down for such discussions, because the impression would be inevitable that a large-scale realignment of exchange rates was in the offing. This takes us back to a question I raised at the beginning of the conference—whether the realignment should come first, followed then by the wider band and the gliding parity, or whether we should rely on the wider band and the gliding parity to bring about the necessary realignment. I submit that the latter possibility exists only where the misalignment is not greater than, let's say, 10 percent; where the misalignment is greater than this, an initial realignment would be needed.

Alvin Hansen offered us a very neat technique for making the transition. He suggested that the United States should invite all official holders of dollars to present them to the U.S. Treasury, which would honor the demand to the last ounce of gold. With the gold gone, the dollar could float. Alvin added that the floating should not be without official management. Initially, of course, the management would be in only one direction, because the United States could only buy, not sell, foreign currencies, but later on it could manage the rate in both directions.

I must say that, for me, this idea has a great attraction. Indeed, it is very similar to a scheme I once proposed myself. Yet I find myself of two minds on this matter, because another attractive possibility would be to stop converting dollars while we still have some gold. If we can assume a framework of international cooperation, or if such cooperation were to be restored a year or two after a serious break in existing arrangements, it might be good to enter negotiations with a little gold on hand. That is not because it is really needed, but because some people believe it is needed. I think Eddie Bernstein once said that it is always good to have a pile of gold when you sit down to have monetary negotiations. The concept of international cooperation has great appeal. I might add, however, that Harry Johnson once asked why—since economic cooperation is only needed while we have the existing lousy system—we should retain that lousy system in order to provide a need for continued cooperation!

One of the most important theoretical points of this conference with regard to flexible rates was made by Walter

Salant. Walter stated that, under fixed exchange rates, adjustment is a burden chiefly for the deficit country, whereas under flexible rates the main burden would be shifted to the surplus country. It was interesting to hear Fred Bergsten pick up the point and say that this shifting of the burden is exactly what would be needed for the so-called dilemma cases in international adjustment. If, in a dilemma case, the deficit country is one that at the same time has unemployment—and therefore should avoid deflation—then this shifting of the burden to the surplus country seems very appropriate.

While still on the subject of flexible exchange rates, I should say a word about optimal currency areas. Since the author of the concept is in the room, it may be impertinent for me to say anything about this matter. As your moderator, however, I will take the chance. First of all, I believe that no one thinks of a system of flexible exchange rates as involving a compulsory flexibility for all 111 members of the IMF. People who argue against flexibility by pointing to the impossibility of having 110 exchange rates change every day are arguing against no one. We can take it for granted that there will be a limited number of currency areas. On the meaning of the word "optimum" in this context, I would observe that, just as the optimum rate of output is usually left to the individual firm and the optimum rate of consumption to the individual consumer, we might leave the question of the optimum size of a currency area to the nations involved. In other words, the optimum size is what those nations believe to be the optimum—a definition which, I believe, is in accord with the proposition made earlier this afternoon by Professor Oliver. Oliver defined an optimum currency area as the area in which we can expect complete harmonization of policies. If two or three countries believe that, together, they constitute one optimum currency area, then they will harmonize their policies; to the extent that they fail to do so, they are not an optimum currency area.

I would grant that there are other ways in which one could define the optimum. For example, if in the 1860's the war between the states had turned out differently, the South would have regarded its area as an optimum currency area, and we might have had an entirely different development over the last hundred years. Incidentally, none of us, I think, would have the temerity to assert that this would have been either worse or better for the South. Such judgments are very difficult to make, ex post as much as ex ante. Perhaps we may reasonably say that, for the North and South together, it was better to remain together, but how the gain from remaining together has been distributed between the two regions is beyond anybody to say.

I come now to the debate between Paul Samuelson and Walter Salant on the question of whether the dollar is overvalued. As you recall, Samuelson said that the dollar has been overvalued for many years, and Salant countered by asking how we could call it overvalued when so many people in the meantime have acquired dollars at the existing price.

Let me say that this is mainly a semantic question. What do we mean by "overvalued"? The term could mean that the market value is such-and-such, but that you or I disagree with the market. I often say that a particular corporate stock is overvalued, because I believe it *is* overvalued. Or the term overvaluation could refer to a currency that is priced too high in relation to statistical evidence about price-level relationships at home and abroad. Or, again, one might say that a currency is overvalued if the fixed exchange rate can be maintained only by foreign official purchases of that currency. If we use this last definition, then clearly Samuelson is right, because monetary authorities all over the world have had to purchase dollars; otherwise, the dollar would have fallen in price.

MUNDELL: What if the monetary authorities want to purchase them?

MACHLUP: We have here a problem of further refinement of the definition. We could use as a fourth concept the Mundell criterion that the dollar is overvalued only if foreign monetary authorities acquire dollars with reluctance. But on that definition, the dollar has been overvalued for a good many years, since several monetary authorities have increased their holdings of dollars in recent years with considerable reluctance.

Let me now switch from exchange-rate questions to the subject of our deliberations today—in particular, to the question of trade controls versus controls on capital movement. Of course, some may think that the choice between trade controls and capital controls is not a very attractive choice. One of the great bonuses distributed by this conference was Leonard Silk's reference to the dilemma a person faces when confronted with a choice between one or two eggs in his beer—if he is allergic to eggs.

Be this as it may, trade controls were defended by Richard Gardner, Gardner Patterson, and Henry Wallich, and were attacked by Gottfried Haberler and, with almost religious fervor, by Randall Hinshaw. Several members, while not attracted to either form of control, expressed a preference for capital controls. Among the reasons put forward for this preference was a belief that capital controls might be more acceptable politically. Legal acceptability, in the sense of consistency with the IMF Articles of Agreement, was also mentioned. Another reason cited was the conviction that vested interests would latch on to trade controls much more tenaciously than to capital controls. For this reason, Haberler preferred capital controls, because he felt that they would be more promptly dismantled.

My own feelings on this issue are somewhat mixed. I am disturbed by the notion that capital movements are somehow less "structural" than the flow of commodities. I submit that they are just as structural. A country like the United States that generates a great deal of savings and that has a capital-labor ratio much higher than any other country is structurally a capital-exporting country. For such a country to hold that it can stop its capital outflow and have a capital inflow for the next ten years or so seems to me entirely untenable. I would also have grave doubts about any cost-benefit analysis which came to the conclusion that capital controls are less harmful than trade controls, because the allocation of capital among the countries of the world has an enormous bearing on the growth of the world economy and on the efficiency in the use of capital in the world at large. We are much too inclined, I am afraid, to underestimate the cost of interfering with the most efficient international allocation of capital. It is a cost element of the first order.

I am not at all convinced that obstacles to capital movement are easily dismantled, as has been suggested. The United States still has the restrictions on foreign lending and on direct investment that it introduced five years ago as a "temporary" stop-gap measure. France has not dismantled the restrictions on capital exports which she introduced thirty years ago, and she has recently started to apply them more strictly. There are several countries in Western Europe that have not had any large deficits in their payments balances for many years but have nevertheless maintained their restrictions on capital movements.

It is quite likely, however, that trade restrictions are more injurious to economic welfare than capital restrictions of the same "effectiveness" (in terms of the net effects on the balance of payments). This is largely a hunch; I have no evidence for its truth or probability value, nor would I know how to obtain conclusive evidence. One of the problems is that the comparative welfare loss for the country resorting to restrictions may be quite different from that of other countries hurt by them. Moreover, quite different countries may be hurt by the two kinds of restrictions. Trade restrictions of country A may hurt A and also B, C, and D; restrictions on capital may hurt A and also X, Y, and Z. A cosmopolitan cost-benefit analyst would, no doubt, reach conclusions quite different from those of a nationalist partisan of any one of the countries concerned, especially an economic adviser to the government of country A.

Underlying the problem of estimating the comparative welfare loss—and thinking for the moment just of the country resorting to the restrictions—is the problem of estimating the net effects upon the balance of payments over a period of several years. If, by means of quotas, we shut out imports having a value of $100 million, will our trade balance improve by $80 million, $50 million, or only $20 million? If we cut out capital exports amounting to $100 million, will the trade balance deteriorate by $10 million, $40 million, or perhaps $90 million? The answers depend, of course, on many things—chiefly on repercussions and feedback effects, many of which will be different according to which other countries are affected and in what ways.

I recall that Richard Cooper has wrestled with this problem, but without conclusive results. The most persuasive argument in support of the assertion that capital restrictions are less harmful than trade restrictions is that capital movements are sometimes diverted in odd ways by existing government measures (including special taxation, divergent inflation rates, and inappropriate exchange rates), so that new restrictions on capital movement need not always lead away from the optimum allocation of resources as determined by "genuine" differences in marginal efficiency. However, in many instances, the controls and restrictions on capital movement are clearly counterproductive from practically every possible point of view. Just imagine for a moment what would have happened if Britain had effectively restricted the export of capital in the nineteenth century. The whole world would be much poorer today.

Most economists pronouncing on adjustment or correction of imbalances of payments have a rather definite preference scale in mind when they are choosing from the arsenal of weapons at the disposal of the authorities. The ordering in this scale is not necessarily the same with regard to the removal of surpluses and the removal of deficits. For example, "liberalization"—the abolition or relaxation of controls and restrictions on trade and capital movement—ranks very high, perhaps in the top position, in recommendations to surplus countries. (As a matter of fact, as Cooper has said, differential liberalization substituted for the poor, or nonexisting, adjustment mechanism in the period from 1950 to 1960.) "Deliberalization"—that is, the imposition or tightening of controls and restrictions—ranks lower among the alternative measures recommended to deficit countries. As another example, monetary expansion or inflation is prescribed for surplus countries with less hesitation than monetary contraction or deflation for deficit countries. This is understandable, since deflation—especially the type that results in serious and protracted unemployment—is the most costly of all the measures at our disposal, although it is still prescribed by some die-hards under the euphemistic name of "monetary discipline."

Where does exchange-rate adjustment stand in this ranking? If the diagnosis is "fundamental disequilibrium" causing chronic deficits in the balance of payments, devaluation or depreciation of the currency is, by almost general accord, given top place among the remedies at our disposal. Deliberalization ranks next, and deflation is the least acceptable alternative. In the prescriptions for chronic surpluses, liberalization is given top honors, followed by up-valuation or appreciation of the currency, with inflation at the bottom of the list. Thus, for deficit as well as for surplus countries, exchange-rate adjustment is preferred to aggregate-demand adjustment.

If economists, government officials, and business executives agree by and large on this ranking—except, perhaps, for the place of liberalization—why is there so much disagreement on the therapies prescribed in particular situations? The differences of opinion lie in the diagnosis of the trouble. What economists judge to be "fundamental disequilibrium," many men in business and government usually pronounce to be a "temporary disturbance" that will yield to proper treatment or will disappear in due course without any treatment. The treatment in question, in the case of a payments deficit, may be mild fiscal and monetary restraint, perhaps disinflation or "cooling off," but without any genuine deflation being required. And since it is believed that the disturbance will soon "go away," temporary controls and restrictions may be prescribed as a stop-gap.

This is a rather characteristic division of opinion. Why are the men in charge of decision-making apt to be more sanguine about an imbalance than the disinterested specialists? One may liken this conflict of opinion to that between a surgeon who urges a radical operation as the only reasonable action, and his patient who is convinced that he will regain his health without the operation. (The analogy is misleading in that the economic adviser does not get paid for the operation, and thus cannot be suspected of a pecuniary bias in favor of surgery.) The optimism which induces the decision-makers to refuse or postpone exchange-rate surgery is to a large extent a function of their fear of pain during and after the operation. The concern of the economist, warning against postponement, is the result of his conviction of the inevitability of the operation and of his assessment of the cost of delaying it.

I do not mean to assert that the economists are always right and the practitioners and officials always wrong. There have been instances in which economists advised or urged exchange-rate adjustment, while the governments proved that they were able to weather the storm and restore balance without unfixing exchange rates. On the other hand, there is clear evidence from time to time of the huge cost of postponing exchange-rate adjustment—I mention only the delays in the devaluation of sterling and in the up-valuation of the German mark. In view of the high cost of delaying necessary adjustment, the present discussion of how to move toward greater flexibility of exchange rates is of paramount importance.

One more point. Resistance to currency devaluation or depreciation is often explained by the contention that the deficit in the balance of payments has been caused by inflation, and could be removed by stopping the inflation. There is, of course, an important difference between an ongoing inflation and an arrested one. But the arrested inflation will usually have had its effects on prices and wage rates (relative to those abroad), and the halt in the inflation does not undo these effects—unless the other countries conveniently inflate at a brisk pace. Hence, realignment of exchange rates will still be required.

In the case of an ongoing inflation, to put off exchange-rate adjustment until after the inflation is halted may be a very poor policy, because it requires a cumbersome and expensive machinery of controls and restrictions, and results in progressive distortions in the economic structure of the country. Even if it is true that devaluation may accelerate the inflation, the effects of the ever-increasing misalignment of the exchange rate are likely to be more injurious to the economy than the price inflation itself. In other words, while greater flexibility of exchange rates may be *highly recommended* for countries with relatively modest deviations from the utopian ideal of "harmonization" of all relevant rates of change, it is almost *imperative* for countries that are "doing their own thing," especially about the rate of increase of their money supply.

APPENDIX: FLEXIBLE EXCHANGE RATES AND INTERNATIONAL ADJUSTMENT

Summary and conclusions

The recent crisis in the foreign exchange markets has resulted in widespread criticism of the present exchange system. The justification for a system of fixed parities is that it contributes to monetary and economic stability. When a country has excessive demand, imports will increase relative to exports and thus hold down the rise in domestic prices. When a country has deficient demand, exports will increase relative to imports and thus hold up production. It is basic to the system of fixed parities that balance-of-payments deficits or surpluses should be temporary and should be eliminated promptly. If the balance of payments cannot be restored without deflation, the parity can be changed with the approval of the Fund. It is at this point, according to the critics, that the system of fixed parities breaks down. Large countries will not change their parities, and the retention of overvalued and undervalued currencies encourages speculation and generates foreign exchange crises.

The advocates of fluctuating exchange rates argue that policies should be determined with reference to the domestic economic situation and not the balance of payments. The easiest way of maintaining balance in international payments is through fluctuating exchange rates. A large and persistent payments deficit usually indicates that a country has inflated demand. A fluctuating rate would restore balance in the exchange market, but only by turning the inflation inward on prices and costs. Unless the inflation is halted, the exchange rate would continue to depreciate; and if the depreciation stimulated speculative capital movements, it would run ahead of domestic inflation, thus intensifying and accelerating it. If the inflation is halted, the balance of payments could be restored with fixed parities suitably adjusted to a country's competitive position.

It may be possible to combine greater flexibility of exchange rates with a high degree of stability over short periods. One method of doing this would be to permit exchange rates to move through a wider range, say, 2 percent on either side of dollar parity. Such a degree of flexibility would help in balance of payments adjustments without stimulating speculative capital movements. A wider range, say, 5 percent, would encourage speculation, and once the exchange rate fell to the lower limit, the flexibility would be exhausted. Another proposal is to permit countries to change their parities by 1 or 2 percent in the course of a year. Although any one year's change could not have much effect in adjusting the balance of payments, the cumulative effect over a period of four or five years could be considerable. The movable parity could be combined with a wider band of about 2 percent without losing some of the benefits of relatively stable exchange rates.

Flexible exchange rates could be helpful in correcting a small or moderate payments deficit. They would be useless in correcting a large and persistent deficit which is the result of inflated demand. Without appropriate domestic measures, the flexibility provided by a wider band or by movable parities could be quickly exhausted. It may be that we live in a world of perpetual inflation. In such a world, a flexible exchange-rate system may be necessary, not because it is inherently better than a fixed-rate system, but because it may be better suited to a world with an inflation bias. If the United States could halt the inflation, there would be no reason for changing the present system of fixed parities.

Present system of fixed parities

The recent crisis in the foreign exchange markets has raised again the question whether a system of fixed parities is suited to the economic realities of the modern world. The Articles of Agreement of the International Monetary Fund, adopted at Bretton Woods in July 1944, contain the following provisions regarding parities of currencies and the range of exchange rates:

> Article IV, Section 1. The par value of the currency of each member shall be expressed in terms of gold as a common denominator or in terms of the U.S. dollar of the weight and fineness in effect on July 1, 1944.

> Article IV, Section 3. The maximum and minimum rates for exchange transactions between the currencies of members . . . shall not differ from parity (i) in the case of spot exchange transactions, by more than one per cent. . . .
>
> Article IV, Section 5 (b). A change in the par value of a member's currency may be made only on the proposal of the member and only after consultation with the Fund. . . . (f) The Fund shall concur in a proposed change . . . if it is satisfied that the change is necessary to correct a fundamental disequilibrium [in the balance of payments].

In essence, the objective at Bretton Woods was to retain the fixed parity aspect of the gold standard while abandoning the rigidities imposed by the traditional gold standard. Although countries had to establish par values for their currencies in terms of gold, the parities were no longer immutable. The Fund agreement contemplated a change in the established parity if this was necessary as an alternative to deflation or to imposing controls on current trade and other payments. However, a change in parity could be made only if the payments deficit was expected to endure. To meet temporary deficits, the Fund had large resources of gold and currencies that were to be used, according to Article I (v) "to give confidence to members . . . thus providing them with opportunity to correct maladjustments in their balance of payments without resorting to measures destructive of national or international prosperity." The requirement of consultation and approval was designed to prevent a change in parity from being excessive and having disruptive effects on the pattern of international payments.

The present system of fixed parities has itself been criticized as a source of instability in a broader sense. Fluctuations in exchange rates are so limited that they can have only a minimal effect in adjusting the balance of payments. The use of reserves and reserve credits on a large scale and over an extended period may cause the imbalance to become embedded in the structure of the economy. When this occurs, there may be no other means of restoring a balanced pattern of international payments except through a change in the parity, a difficult step for large trading countries. The protracted delay in restoring the balance of payments encourages speculative capital movements on such a massive scale as to threaten the international monetary system. According to the critics, this is what happened in the recent exchange crisis. The solution that they envisage is a greater degree of flexibility in exchange rates—either freely fluctuating rates, wider margins from parity, or gradually changing parities. Surpluses and deficits would be permitted to manifest themselves in changes in exchange rates that would facilitate the restoration of a balanced pattern of international payments.

It is no answer to the critics to say that the system of fixed parities is an old tradition, that it has been in operation in its present form for over twenty years, and that for these reasons it should be continued as it is. The system of fixed parities does not derive ultimate validity from its former relationship to the gold standard or its adoption at Bretton Woods. If the present exchange system is to be retained, the justification must be that it contributes to the achievement of a stable and prosperous world economy. If it does not serve that purpose, and particularly if it has become a source of instability and destructive of national and international prosperity, as the critics say, then a new system of exchange rates should be adopted by the members of the Fund.

The rationale of fixed but adjustable parities

The present system of fixed parities, adjustable with the approval of the Fund, is usually defended as necessary for the growth of world trade and investment. Fluctuating exchange rates would add another element of uncertainty in international payments. The uncertainty could be met through forward exchange transactions. But if exchange rates can fluctuate to a significant extent, and that is the purpose of flexible rates, then the risk of larger fluctuations would raise the cost of forward cover. Even with the present system, the cost of forward cover may rise to 5 percent or more a year. This is an infrequent occurrence with fixed parities; it may be more common with fluctuating exchange rates. In any case, this is not a decisive argument in favor of fixed parities.

The justification for a system of fixed parities is that it contributes to monetary and economic stability in a more fundamental sense. In any free economy, home demand will grow at an uneven rate, with a large increase in a period of expansion and little or no increase in a period of recession. When a country has a rapid increase of home demand, this will encourage an increase of output, but it will also result in an increase of imports of goods and services relative to exports. Thus, in a period of expansion, a system of fixed parities induces an increase of the supply of goods and services relative to home demand, and minimizes the domestic price and cost inflation. There is a dramatic illustration of this aspect of fixed parities in the United States in recent years. From 1964 to 1968, the U.S. balance on goods and services fell by $6 billion because of the inflation of home demand. If there had not been such an enormous increase of imports relative to exports, all of the excessive demand would have had to be absorbed in an even greater rise of domestic prices and costs.

Similarly, when a country with a fixed parity is in a recession because of an inadequate growth of home demand, the effect on production and employment will be moderated by an increase of exports of goods and services relative to imports. This happened on a large scale in Germany between 1965 and 1967. In constant prices, output (GNP) increased by 2.3 percent in 1966 and was virtually unchanged in 1967. The export surplus, however, rose sharply in both years. In the boom year 1965, net exports were –0.1 percent of the gross national product; in 1966, net exports were 1.4 percent of the gross national product; and in the recession year 1967, net exports were 3.3 percent of the gross national product. Even without allowance for the multiplier effect, the increase in the export surplus between 1965 and 1967 was a major factor in preventing a serious recession from emerging in Germany.

The stabilizing effect of fixed parities depends on the capacity of the world economy to absorb part of the change in domestic demand when a country has a boom or recession. As no country accounts for more than 15 percent of world trade, the impact of the change in exports relative to imports in one country can be spread over a vast amount of trade of many other countries. Of course, this is true only when cyclical fluctuations in the large industrial countries are independent, as they have generally been in the postwar period. When the economic conjuncture is coincident in the large industrial countries, changes in the export surplus can help one country only by hurting another. At such a time, coordinated policies of expansion or restraint are necessary. Such policies might have uneven effects on different countries. But the availability of adequate reserves should make it possible to pursue such policies without too much concern about temporary effects on the balance of payments.

It is basic to the system of fixed parities that balance-of-payments deficits or surpluses should be temporary—that they should ordinarily be the result of cyclical fluctuations out of phase with those of other countries. Under such conditions, a slowdown of a too-rapid expansion in the deficit country or an acceleration of a too-retarded expansion in the surplus country would restore the balance of payments. The adjustment process would be completely in harmony with the needs of domestic policy—to prevent inflation in the deficit country and to avoid recession in the surplus country. Of course, countries may not take the measures necessary for adjusting the balance of payments, and surpluses and deficits may become large and persistent. If this is permitted to happen, the deficit or surplus may become embedded in the structure of the economy.

When the deficit or surplus in the balance of payments cannot be eliminated by acceptable domestic policies designed to restore economic growth with monetary stability, an enduring change has occurred in the relative economic position of the country. It may be due to an inflation that has resulted in an excessive rise in prices and costs in the deficit country. It may be due to a change in reciprocal demand for exports and imports between a surplus country and the rest of the world. In either case, the remedy under the Bretton Woods system is not to deflate the economy of the deficit country or to inflate the economy of the surplus country, but to change the parities of the currencies.

It is at this point, according to the critics, that the system of fixed parities breaks down. The great trading countries, it is said, are not willing to change the parities of their currencies in order to adjust the balance of payments. A devaluation in a deficit country is a confession of persistent error in domestic policy, an unpalatable admission for any government; and in spite of the blessing of the Fund, it may be regarded as impairing the prestige of the country that resorts to it. Revaluation, that is, appreciation of the parity by a surplus country, is firmly resisted by exporters who do not wish to surrender the trading advantage they derive from an undervalued currency. Thus, changes in parity are rarely used, and the insistence on retaining overvalued and undervalued currencies generates foreign exchange crises.

Until recently, it would have been said that the Fund had succeeded in maintaining a system of fixed parities with agreed changes when necessary. True, there have been only eight changes in parity by large industrial countries since the devaluations of 1949, of which two were the appreciation of the mark and guilder in 1961. This shows, however, that a reasonably well-balanced pattern of international payments (the special case of the United States excepted) was established between 1950 and 1964. The argument that large industrial countries cannot or will not change parities rests on developments since 1964. The delay in devaluing sterling and the unwillingness of Germany to appreciate the mark undoubtedly aggravated the imbalance in international payments. The recent exchange crisis has shown that changes in parity to eliminate a persistent deficit or surplus are not undertaken as readily as contemplated at Bretton Woods.

It is impossible to avoid persistent payments deficits and surpluses if countries do not act promptly to prevent or halt inflation. Fixed parities are best suited for a world that is prepared to combine economic growth with monetary stability. Theoretically, if inflation were at the same pace in all large industrial countries, it would still be possible to have international balance. In practice, in-step inflation is unlikely, if for no other reason than the different response that may be expected from the same proportionate excess of aggregate demand. In a world willing to combine economic growth with monetary stability, fixed parities can help in achieving this objective. Even with domestic price and cost stability, properly defined, it would still be necessary to adjust parities when a structural change alters the reciprocal demand for exports and imports.

One of the common arguments in favor of fixed parities is that it will induce countries to follow domestic policies conducive to monetary stability. Unfortunately, recent experience does not bear this out. When a country can finance a persistent deficit because its currency will be held as reserves by other countries (the case of the United States) or because massive reserve credits will be provided by international institutions or by other countries (the case of the United Kingdom), the dampening effect of the balance-of-payments deficit on domestic prices and costs may encourage a country to delay taking the necessary corrective measures. It is possible that a system of fluctuating exchange rates would be more effective in inducing countries to follow appropriate domestic policies. If inflation manifests itself in a depreciation of the exchange rate, governments may feel under greater compulsion to halt the inflation than if the effect is seen solely in a fall of reserves which can be disguised or massive reserve debts which are not shown in the reserve position. However, if governments are not willing to follow appropriate domestic policies simply to avoid inflation, it is doubtful whether they will be compelled to do this by any system of exchange rates—whether fixed parities or fluctuating rates.

Fluctuating exchange rates

The policy of fluctuating exchange rates was widely used during the 1930's, but it was regarded as an aberration that had to be tolerated during the great depression rather than as a new instrument for facilitating balance-of-payments adjustment. In an attempt to maintain the gold standard in the 1930's, countries adopted strong deflationary policies—contracting the money supply at a time of widespread unemployment. The deflationary policies were a complete failure. They intensified the depression and did not save the gold standard. It was only after the United Kingdom and the United States abandoned the gold standard and adopted a policy of expansion that the recovery began. The gold bloc (France, the Netherlands, Belgium, and Switzerland) remained on the gold standard until 1936, despite the increasing pressure from the devaluations of other currencies which intensified their unemployment. The best that can be said for the system of fluctuating exchange rates as it actually operated in the 1930's is that competitive depreciation was far better than competitive deflation.

The gold bloc could not continue to maintain fixed gold parities in the face of the large depreciation of the dollar and the pound. When deepening depression compelled France to change the gold parity of the franc in 1936, it was done after consultation with the United States and the United Kingdom. At the same time, the three countries declared their agreement on a policy of restoring fixed parities. The Netherlands, Belgium, and Switzerland also devalued their currencies and adhered to the Tripartite Declaration. A completely new set of fixed parities emerged in the 1930's quite different from the historic parities under the old gold standard. The outbreak of war prevented the full implementation of the Tripartite Declaration; but its principles of fixed parities, with changes only after international consultation, became the basis of the Bretton Woods system.

The advocates of fluctuating exchange rates argue that policies should be determined with reference to the domestic economy and not with reference to the balance of payments, which is a minor sector of the economy. In the United States, for example, exports of goods and services in 1967 comprised 5.8 percent of gross national production, and imports of goods and services comprised 5.2 percent of gross national expenditure. To determine policy on the basis of the balance of payments is a case of the tail wagging the dog. In fact, of course, policy is not made solely with reference to the balance of payments—either in the United States or in other countries. Moreover, the advocates of fluctuating exchange rates imply that there is a necessary conflict between domestic and international objectives which actually seldom exists. Good policy for the balance of payments is generally, although not always, good policy for the domestic economy.

Persistent balance-of-payments deficits and surpluses are ordinarily the result of too rapid expansion or inadequate growth. Thus, measures to restrain the economy when there is a payments deficit or to stimulate the economy when there is a payments surplus are consistent with stability and growth of the economy as well as balance in international payments. That is obviously true in the United States and Germany, the major deficit and surplus countries at this time. The Bretton Woods principles are the very opposite of those implied in the criticism that countries must follow policies undesirable for the domestic economy because of the balance of payments. A member of the Fund is not expected to deflate its economy (as distinguished from halting the inflation) in order to restore its balance of payments. On the contrary, it can propose a change in parity, and the Fund cannot object merely on the grounds that deflation would be the better alternative. Unfortunately, in practice, countries neither deflate nor devalue, but seem inclined to place greater reliance on direct controls affecting trade, other current transactions, and international investment.

On the positive side, the advocates of fluctuating exchange rates argue that, with such a policy, the exchange market would automatically maintain a balance in a country's international payments. It is implicit in this argument that the real source of trouble is the payments deficit and not the economic conditions which give rise to the deficit. This may be true, in a sense, in the rare case where a deficit is due to a structural change in a country's relative international economic position. It is not at all true in the common case where the balance-of-payments deficit is due to excessive domestic demand. In a system of fluctuating exchange rates, a country suffering from inflation will find the exchange rate for its currency depreciating in order to prevent an excess of imports over exports of goods and services. As all of the excessive domestic demand will be turned inward, the probability is that in the long run the rise of prices will be greater with fluctuating exchange rates than with fixed parities, unless measures to halt the inflation are taken more promptly because of the obvious depreciation of the currency in the exchange market.

The advocates of fluctuating exchange rates usually assume that the depreciation in the exchange market will be no more than a reflection of relative inflation of prices and costs. This would be so if the behavior of exchange rates had no effect on the speculative movement of short-term funds. In practice, however, the gradual fall of the exchange rate of a currency would stimulate an outflow of funds in anticipation of further depreciation. Under such conditions, with depreciation running ahead of domestic inflation, the depreciation would itself become a cause of intensified inflation. For the exchange rate would not merely achieve a balance in the normal current and capital accounts, but a surplus equal to the outflow of short-term funds. Because of this, the country with inflation would be deprived of some of its output of goods and services, thus intensifying the price effects of excessive domestic demand. Furthermore, the greater depreciation would raise the prices of import and export goods more than would be justified by domestic demand, and might lead to offsetting wage increases that accelerate the inflation.

In the rest of the world, an inflow of speculative funds from abroad would be equally disruptive for the domestic economy. The speculative inflow would cause an appreciation of the currency in the exchange market and result in a deficit in the balance of payments on current and ordinary capital account. In order to offset the contracting effect of an increased import surplus of goods and services, the monetary authorities would have to expand domestic demand. Furthermore, if the speculative inflow were suddenly halted, because the inflation was brought to an end by the other country, the currency would depreciate, the balance on goods and services would be reversed, and the monetary authorities would have to undertake an offsetting contraction to avoid an excess of domestic demand. The problem would be even more acute if the speculative movement of funds were reversed instead of merely being halted. In brief, management of the domestic economy would not be easier under a system of fluctuating exchange rates if the world economy was being subjected to inflation in a great trading country.

The difficulties that countries now have with movements of short-term funds would probably be greatly intensified under a system of fluctuating rates. The argument frequently made by central bankers that fluctuating exchange rates really mean sinking exchange rates is an expression of the view that they would generate much larger and more haphazard speculative movements of short-term funds. For a country like the United States, with enormous foreign holdings of liquid dollar assets, the danger of large speculative movements of funds (inward as well as outward) in anticipation of fluctuations in the rate of exchange is especially great. With fluctuating exchange rates, the U.S. economy might be subjected to more inflationary and deflationary pressures, arising particularly from speculative capital movements, than is possible under a system of fixed parities.

It may be said that this criticism of fluctuating exchange rates is mainly based on the assumption that they will intensify speculative capital movements. That is so, and it is a reasonable assumption if countries permit inflation to continue under a system of fluctuating exchange rates. Obviously, speculative capital movements would be small, perhaps no more than with fixed rates, if governments maintain domestic monetary stability. But if governments are prepared to follow such policies, they can adjust their balance of payments just as well with fixed parities as with fluctuating exchange rates. If countries need fluctuating exchange rates, after a prolonged inflation, in order to test the exchange market before establishing a new parity, they can do that now under the Bretton Woods system. The Fund has been generous in accepting fluctuating rates as an interim measure until inflation is halted, and it is clear that a new parity appropriate to the state of the economy can be proposed, approved, and made effective.

Wider margins above and below parity

Even if the monetary authorities are not prepared to accept fluctuating exchange rates, they might secure some help in adjusting the balance of payments if greater flexibility were provided through widening the margins of exchange-rate movements beyond the 1 percent from parity established at Bretton Woods. The question of widening the margins for exchange-rate fluctuation, while retaining a fixed parity, first arose during the 1920's prior to the restoration of the gold standard by the United Kingdom. Keynes suggested at that time that the spread between the buying and selling price for gold should be widened to 1/2 percent or 1 percent. This would not have added much to the flexibility of exchange rates—in fact, not as much as was later provided at Bretton Woods. As the gold points were about 0.4 percent above and below parity for dollar-sterling exchange, even a 1 percent difference in the buying and selling price of gold would have permitted exchange rates to fluctuate by less than 1 percent from parity.

The same question arose in the United States when the gold standard was restored in January 1934. The Gold Reserve Act of 1934 established a new gold value of the dollar at $35 an ounce. The Treasury was authorized to impose a handling charge of 1/4 percent for buying or selling gold. The effect was to widen the gold export and import points, which set the limits of fluctuation in the exchange rates, by 1/2 percent. With the cost of shipping gold between Western Europe and the United States, the gold points were about 3/4 percent above and below parity. This is the margin that most central banks still prefer.

Prior to the Bretton Woods conference, the possibility of establishing wider margins was discussed once more. In the *Questions and Answers on the International Monetary Fund*, issued by the U.S. Treasury on June 10, 1944, the U.S. technical experts stated their views in these terms:

> It is too much to hope that even a relatively broad range, say 2 percent [on either side of parity], within which member currencies might be permitted to fluctuate would provide sufficient flexibility for adjusting a country's international balance of payments through a movement in exchange rates. There will, nevertheless, be seasonal or even small cyclical pressures [on the balance of payments] that can be considerably offset by a movement of exchange rates within such a broad range prescribed by the Fund.
>
> There is to this extent something to be said even on the economic side [as distinguished from the administration of Fund resources] for broadening the range of exchange rates prescribed by the Fund as compared with the old spread between gold points. On the other hand, the permissible variations must not introduce a risk of exchange fluctuations so considerable as to deter short-term financing of international trade or long-term lending for investment. Neither should the permissible fluctuation encourage speculation of a character that would tend to weaken the established structure of exchange rates, or too easily introduce a disrupting influence in the money and exchange markets.

The Bretton Woods conference decided to establish the limit of exchange-rate fluctuations at 1 percent above and below parity. Nevertheless, it is possible that a wider margin of 2 percent on either side of parity would facilitate balance-of-payments adjustments under certain conditions, particularly if the margin were measured with respect to a single currency, such as the dollar. A deficit country (other than the United States) could allow the exchange rate for its currency to fall to 2 percent below dollar parity; and a surplus country (other than the United States) could allow the exchange rate for its currency to rise to 2 percent above dollar parity. Thus, the exchange rates between any two currencies, other than the dollar, could actually be 4 percent different from their cross-rate dollar parities. The exchange rate for the dollar with any currency could never be more than 2 percent above or below parity, but even this would provide somewhat more leeway for the United States than the present limit of 1 percent, although not as much as other countries could secure from a wider margin of 2 percent in the dollar exchange rate of their currencies.

Such a limited degree of exchange flexibility could have little effect on the balance of payments when there is a large and persistent deficit or surplus. When the deficit is moderate and due to ordinary cyclical forces or to minor structural changes in the relative international economic position of a country, a shift in the exchange rate to the lower limit in the deficit country and the upper limit in the surplus country could help to adjust the balance of payments. Some of the substitute devices, such as changes in import charges or in export rebates, which came out of the recent exchange crisis, probably have no more effect on the balance of payments than could be achieved through a movement of exchange rates within a 2 percent band on either side of dollar parity, particularly as the rise or fall in exchange rates would apply to services as well as to exports and imports. Of course, where the payments deficit is due to inflated home demand, such minor changes in exchange rates could have no effect in improving the balance of payments unless the inflation were halted.

On the capital side, a 2 percent margin might hold down speculative movements of short-term funds, provided it reduced expectations of a change in parity. Thus, if Currency A falls to the bottom of the range (98 percent of dollar parity) and Currency B rises to the top of the range (102 percent of dollar parity), a transfer of funds from Country A to Country B would involve paying a premium of about 4 percent. If the situation changes, so that Currency A rises to the top of the range (102 percent of dollar parity) and Currency B falls to the bottom of the range (98 percent of dollar parity), a reversal of the previous outflow of funds would involve a total cost of about 8 percent. This is a high potential cost for taking a short position in Currency A and a long position in Currency B unless there is great expectation of a devaluation or an appreciation. In this respect, the wider margin would operate on speculation in much the same way as a high premium or discount on forward exchange. It would discourage speculative capital movements except when anticipations of a change in parity are very strong.

A still wider range, say 5 percent on either side of parity, might add little real flexibility to the exchange system while undermining confidence in the parity. The 10 percent maximum shift in exchange rates between two currencies (other than the dollar) is more than is necessary to keep cyclical deficits within reasonable limits. Where the deficit is large and persistent and is due to inflated demand, even a fall in the exchange rate to 5 percent below dollar parity might not be sufficient to restore the balance of payments. And if the deficit is due to a significant change in the relative international economic position, the exchange rate might fall to the lower limit and stay there indefinitely. This would exhaust the flexibility that the wider range is intended to provide. Furthermore, it would be very difficult for a currency to return to parity, or above it, after it had once fallen to the lower limit of a 5 percent margin and stayed there for a time. The lower exchange rate would soon become embedded in the structure of the economy, and a return to parity would create much the same difficulties that surplus countries seem to have in undertaking a revaluation of their currencies.

Moreover, a wider band than 2 percent might itself generate excessive fluctuations in exchange rates that could prove disruptive. If exchange rates could move within a 5 percent band around dollar parity, a fall in the exchange rate by 1 percent or so below parity would encourage expectations that the fall would continue until the rate reached the lower limit. The risk in selling a currency for which the exchange rate has fallen by 1 percent would not be very great. The prospect that the exchange rate would fall to 5 percent below parity, if this is the width of the band, would certainly be much greater than the prospect of an equivalent change in parity at present. Unless the authorities intervened, the speculative outflow of funds would almost certainly force the rate down to the limit. Thus, a very wide band would magnify the problem of disruptive capital movements, and either result in exaggerated and unnecessary exchange-rate fluctuations, or compel the authorities to intervene to minimize fluctuations in exchange rates.

In short, a wider band of about 2 percent on either side of parity probably provides about as much flexibility as is consistent with the expectation that exchange rates will actually move within the permitted range. A wider band of 5 percent might mean more frequent intervention by the monetary authorities on a larger scale to prevent an unnecessary decline in the exchange rate. And where a movement in the exchange rate to this extent is necessary, the flexibility will be exhausted with the first serious payments problem and will be unrestorable thereafter except through a change in parity. It may not be too much to say that when a country does need a 5 percent fall in the exchange rate, the payments problem is one that could be better met by a depreciation—of course, only after domestic measures are taken to make sure that the new rate will be effective. A 5 percent band might make it easier for a surplus country to accept a de facto appreciation of its currency on the grounds that it is not a change in parity and, in any case, was caused by market forces. That may be the most constructive result that could be expected from a band as wide as 5 percent on either side of dollar parity.

Movable parities: the crawling peg

Because too great flexibility of exchange rates, whether freely fluctuating rates or a very wide band, may stimulate speculative capital movements, an alternative has been proposed in the form of movable parities which may be changed by small but predetermined amounts. Under this proposal, a country would be permitted to adjust its parity at the rate of 1 or 2 percent a year, with adjustments made monthly, quarterly, or semi-annually. Although the change in parity in any one year would be very small, the cumulative changes over a period of years would enable a country to move gradually from a parity that overvalues its currency to one appropriate to its relative international economic position. The basic concept is not new, but it has acquired a much more sophisticated form in recent years.

In his *Tract on Monetary Reform* (1923), Keynes discussed

some innovations that could be introduced if the United Kingdom were to return to a gold standard, as it did in 1925. His proposal for a movable peg, combined with wider gold points, was as follows (p. 190):

> The Bank of England should have a buying and a selling price for gold, just as it did before the war, and this price might remain unchanged for considerable periods, just as bank-rate does. But it would not be fixed or pegged once and for all, any more than bank-rate is fixed. The Bank's rate for gold would be announced every Thursday morning at the same time as its rate for discounting bills, with a difference between its buying and selling rates corresponding to the pre-war margin [nearly 1/6 of 1 percent] . . . except that in order to obviate too frequent changes in the rate, the difference might be wider . . . say, 1/2 to 1 percent. A willingness on the part of the Bank both to buy and to sell gold at rates fixed for the time being would keep the dollar-sterling exchange steady within corresponding limits, so that the exchange rate would not move with every breath of wind but only when the Bank had come to a considered judgment that a change was required for the sake of the stability of sterling prices.

There are various ways in which a movable parity could be operated. The simplest would be to permit a country to change the parity agreed upon with the Fund on its own initiative by no more than 1 or 2 percent a year. The size and frequency of the movement in parity would have to be related to the permitted margin of fluctuation above and below parity in order to avoid discontinuous changes in the exchange rate. Thus, if a 2 percent change in parity were permitted each year, the preferred range of exchange rates would be at least 1 percent above and below parity, but could be as much as 2 percent. This would let the exchange rate move to the bottom of the range before the parity was reduced and start at the top of the range when the new parity was established. Between changes in parity, the exchange rate would be permitted to decline gradually to the bottom of the range if another change in the parity would seem to be indicated. If no further change in the parity were needed, the rate would not move to the floor, but would fluctuate within the permitted range—say, 1 or 2 percent from parity.

An alternative proposal is to determine the parity by the average rate of exchange in the market over a preceding period—say, the previous 12 months. Thus, if the exchange rate fell to the bottom of the range, 1 percent below parity, and stayed there for a year, the new parity would be 1 percent below the previous parity. And if the exchange rate then fell again to the bottom of the range, and stayed there, another 1 percent change of parity could be made after a year. The purpose of basing the change in parity on actual experience in the exchange market is to avoid such action unless it is necessary. Presumably, such a test provides a market justification for a change in parity, although the balance of payments and the reserve position of a country provide a much more realistic test of whether a change in parity is really needed.

The case for a movable parity is that small changes could be made without disrupting the money and exchange markets. The expectation of a 1 or 2 percent change in parity, spread out over the course of a year, would not induce an outflow of capital if the interest-rate differential (a higher rate in the country reducing the parity) were in excess of the maximum change. Furthermore, the premium or discount on forward exchange would be relatively moderate if all that could be expected were a change in parity at the rate of 1 or 2 percent a year. In short, even assured changes in parities would not disrupt the money and exchange markets if the changes were relatively small. The real question is whether such a system would facilitate adjustment of the balance of payments.

A 1 or 2 percent change in parity in the course of a year would obviously do little to help a country whose prices and costs were rising by more than this small amount relative to the average of its competitors. And, of course, it could not be a substitute for restraint on the economy where the deficit is due to excess domestic demand. The crawling peg seems best suited to offset the balance-of-payments effect of a creeping cost inflation, without excess demand. It could also be rationalized as a means of offsetting a slowly deteriorating trend in a country's relative international economic position arising from a gradual change in reciprocal demand for exports and imports. In fact, the movable parity is best understood as a case of anticipatory (preventive) devaluation.

The kind of payments problem that undermines the parity—that is, a large and persistent deficit—could not be dealt with through a 1 or 2 percent change in parity each year. Of course, larger changes in parity could be made with the approval of the Fund. The threat of a larger devaluation might still encourage speculative capital movements when the balance of payments becomes very weak. Perhaps the knowledge that a cumulative devaluation of, say, 6 to 8 percent will occur automatically in the next few years, would discourage speculators from betting on a large devaluation very soon and would encourage the monetary authorities to defend the parity pro tem by even greater use of reserves and reserve credit than at present. No doubt, if countries follow appropriate domestic policies, some help in balance-of-payments adjustment could be secured through the additional flexibility provided by a movable parity combined with a somewhat wider range of exchange-rate fluctuation—say, 2 percent on either side of parity.

Flexible exchange rates as an adjustment mechanism

All of the proposals for providing greater flexibility in the present system of fixed parities are designed to be a positive help in adjusting the pattern of international payments. The critics argue that the present adjustment mechanism is not working, that it places too much responsibility on the deficit country, and that exchange-rate flexibility is a substitute for unacceptable domestic policies. Payments deficits have different causes, and flexible exchange rates may or may not be helpful in adjusting the balance of payments in any specific case. For convenience, payments deficits may be classified as due to (a) cyclical fluctuations, (b) persistent excess demand, (c) a loss of competitiveness because of a preceding inflation of prices and costs, or (d) structural changes impairing the relative international economic position of a country. How would flexible exchange rates facilitate adjustment in these cases?

First, a country that has a deficit only when it is in the expansion phase of a business cycle does not really have a payments problem. The test of a payments problem is whether a country has a deficit on an average of good years and bad, with the qualification that the balance of payments over a long period should be in sufficient surplus to provide a country with an appropriate share of the increase of world monetary reserves. A cyclical payments deficit is properly met by using reserves and reserve credit, a policy that will minimize the long-run price and cost effects of a cyclical expansion. That is the rationale of fixed parities supported by the use of reserves.

Second, a country that has a large and persistent deficit because of excess demand cannot solve its payments problem within the framework of any practical degree of exchange flexibility. A depreciation within a wider band cannot restore the balance of payments if the excess demand is allowed to persist. The best proof of this is the experience of the United Kingdom since the devaluation of sterling by 14 percent. This is much more than any flexible system of exchange rates could provide, freely fluctuating rates apart, yet it has not succeeded until now in improving the trade balance. In the first three quarters of 1968, after devaluation, U.K. imports increased by over 6 percent in dollar value and by nearly 24 percent in sterling value compared with 1967.

Third, a country may have a noncompetitive level of prices and costs even when it no longer has excess demand. If prices and costs are not too far out of line with those of competing countries, a really wide band of exchange-rate fluctuation, say, 5 percent, might permit adjustment of the balance of payments without a change in parity. Where the loss of competitiveness is more than 5 percent, the wider band would not meet the problem. A movable peg might restore the competitive position after four or five years, but it would require the use of enormous reserves and reserve credit to support an unsuitable parity while the country crawled toward a balanced payments position.

Fourth, a country may have a gradual deterioration in its international economic position relative to that of other large trading countries. The creation of the Common Market, with preferences for trade among members, is a structural change that has affected reciprocal demand between these countries and the rest of the world. The shift in Germany from a rapid rate of growth until 1965 to a more moderate rate of growth in recent years is a structural change which will probably continue as indicated by the demographic data on the future growth of the labor force. Such structural changes are usually gradual and could be offset by flexible exchange rates or movable parities.

As this brief analysis indicates, flexible exchange rates cannot be a complete substitute for the normal process of adjustment of balance of payments—that is, by restraining expansion in the deficit country and stimulating expansion in the surplus country. Without such domestic measures, the flexibility provided by a wider band or by movable parities would be quickly exhausted. Freely fluctuating rates would, of course, force an elimination of the deficit through depreciation, but it would inevitably intensify the inflation unless appropriate measures were taken to eliminate excess demand. The view that a system of flexible exchange rates provides an easy and painless method of eliminating imbalance in international payments is without foundation. It may ease the process of adjustment in some cases, but it will not be effective unless it is supported by appropriate domestic policies. It may be possible to put off taking corrective measures for a longer time with flexible exchange rates than with fixed parities, but only at the cost of prolonging and perhaps accelerating the inflation. Sooner or later governments must accept responsibility for establishing monetary stability, for domestic reasons if not for balance-of-payments reasons.

It may be that we live in a world of perpetual inflation, although one cannot generalize with certainty on the basis of recent experience. In such a world it will be difficult to maintain a system of fixed parities. If this should be true, a more flexible exchange system may be necessary, not because it is inherently better, but because it may be better suited to a world with an inflation bias. If a more flexible exchange system must be introduced, it would be desirable to retain as much of the short-term stabilizing influence of fixed parities as is consistent with some reliance on changes in exchange rates for balance-of-payments adjustment. A system of gradually moving parities, with a somewhat wider band, perhaps 2 percent on either side of parity, might be the best alternative to fixed parities with exchange-rate fluctuations limited to 1 percent.

The changes in the international monetary system that

would result from limited movable parities and a somewhat wider band of exchange-rate fluctuation need not be great. Exchange rates would still be relatively stable over short periods, and the monetary authorities would continue to intervene in the exchange market to support their currencies when they had reached the lower limit permitted for the time being. The need for monetary reserves would not be substantially less than at present, and an adequate growth of monetary reserves would still be necessary. The dollar would probably have to play an even greater role in the international monetary system. The dollar exchange rate would be the basis for determining the acceptable limits of exchange-rate fluctuation, and the dollar would be the currency with which the monetary authorities intervene in the exchange market.

It would be impossible for gold to have the same universal relationship to currencies if exchange rates could depart considerably from parities and the parities themselves could be moved frequently. Nevertheless, the gold parity of the dollar could and should remain fixed in a system of flexible exchange rates. The danger of a disruptive preference for gold, however, would probably be even greater than at present. Some form of the Reserve Settlement Account would be necessary, with gold, dollars, and Special Drawing Rights used together pro rata in reserve transactions between monetary authorities. If the international monetary system is not to have an inflationary bias with flexible exchange rates, it would be necessary to have a strong dollar and a stable and prosperous U.S. economy. Of course, if the United States could achieve this, there would be no reason for changing the present system of fixed parities.

NAME INDEX

SUBJECT INDEX